JB JOSSEY-BASS™

A Wiley Brand

Profitable Direct Mail Appeals

Planning, Implementing, & Maximizing Results

SECOND EDITION

Scott C. Stevenson, Editor

WILEY

978-1-118-69309-4   ISBN

978-1-118-70435-6   ISBN (online)

Profitable Direct Mail Appeals — 2nd Edition

Planning, Implementing and Maximizing Results

Published by

Stevenson, Inc.

P.O. Box 4528 • Sioux City, Iowa • 51104
Phone 712.239.3010 • Fax 712.239.2166
www.stevensoninc.com

TABLE OF CONTENTS

Chapter 1: **Plan Your Direct Mail Year**.....................4

- *Keep Refining Your Yearlong Direct Mail Appeal Plan*
- *Develop Your Entire Year's Direct Mail Plan*
- *Direct Mail Tip*
- *Evaluating Direct Mail Consultants*
- *Create a System for Coding Appeals*
- *Keep Direct Mail Pieces Simple, User-friendly*
- *How to Make Direct Mailings More Personal*
- *Managing Track Codes on Mailed Appeals*
- *Use Appeal Codes to Track Gifts*
- *Shrewd Direct Mail Planning*

Chapter 2: **Lists and List Management** 9

- *Spend Time Developing Your Mailing List*
- *Building a Mailing List From Scratch or Build on an Existing One*
- *Gather E-mail Addresses*
- *Build a Mailing List of Qualified Names*
- *Turn to Those You Serve for Names*
- *Call Reports Are More Than a Record*
- *Update Lost Addresses*
- *Use Tracer Cards to Locate Lost Constituents*
- *Include Businesses on Your Mailing List*
- *Build Your E-mail Database*
- *How Do You Define Your Solicitable Base?*
- *How to Build a Database of Qualified Prospects*
- *Records Management Tip*
- *Maintain a Summary Sheet in Each Donor File*

Chapter 3: **Segment and Target Key Audiences** 13

- *Mail, E-mail Solicitations Target Young Alumni Donors*
- *Messages to Persuade Lapsed Donors*
- *Anniversary Letters Offer Effective Way of Renewing Support*
- *Segment Past Donors According to Gift Clubs*
- *Turn Sybunts Into Consistent Supporters*
- *Tailor Brochures to Targeted Age Groups*
- *Test Appeals to Non-donors*
- *Generational Segmenting Boosts Response Rate*
- *List Management Tip*
- *Analyze Your Mailing List at Least Annually*
- *Postcards Educate Students on Importance of Philanthropy*
- *Direct Mail Appeals: Donors vs. Non-donors*

Chapter 4: **Writing for Results** 18

- *Write a Simple, Concise Call to Action; Repeat*
- *Inject Compelling Language Into Appeals*
- *Encourage Donors to Move Up to Next Giving Club Level*
- *Writing Effective Appeal Letters*
- *When Writing Marketing Copy*
- *Writing Tips to Make Your Job Easier*
- *Let Your Post Script Say It All*
- *Produce Appeals That Get Results*
- *Useful Elements for Appeal Letters*

- *Gather Testimonials for Direct Mail Appeals*
- *Direct Mail Tip*
- *Combine Stewardship Message With Your Appeal*
- *Consider an Attention-grabbing, Stand-alone Statement*
- *Draft Appeal for Someone You Know*
- *Direct Mail Tip*
- *Overcoming Writer's Block*
- *Personal Stories Provide Powerful Ammunition*
- *Seeking First-time Gifts? Consider Monthly Appeal*
- *Let Donors Write Your Appeals*
- *Phrases That Convey Urgency*
- *Appeal Writing Tips*
- *Direct Mail Tip*
- *Effective Writing Tip*

Chapter 5: **Key Package Components**.....................25

- *Use Response Cards With Direct Mail, Face-to-face Calls*
- *Use Phrases as Envelope Teasers*
- *Envelope Acronyms*
- *Don't Underestimate Value of a Wish List*
- *Check, Then Choose Best Way to Communicate*
- *Include 'In Memory' and 'In Honor of' Opportunities*
- *New Donor Packet Encourages Repeat Giving*
- *Six Alternatives to 'Affix Postage Here'*
- *Mention Online Giving on All Pledge Forms*
- *Avoid Critical Offer Mistakes*
- *Outer Envelope Plays a Role in Response*
- *Include Mission Statement on Pledge Forms*

Chapter 6: **Try and Test New Ideas** 29

- *25 Percent Increase in Programming Justifies Request for Equal Increase in Giving*
- *Try Testing Back-to-back Appeals*
- *Test New Mailing Options*
- *Test Direct Mail Pieces Head to Head*
- *Two Cardinal Rules for Successful Appeals*
- *Add Personalized Brochure in Your Annual Fund Mailings*
- *Survey Reveals Need to Retool Appeal*

Chapter 7: **Improve Your Response Rate** 32

- *Boost Your Appeal's Response Rate With a 'Johnson Box'*
- *Develop Second-time Follow-up Procedures*
- *Direct Mail Tips*
- *Personal Notes Quadruple Letter's Response Rate*
- *Create Appeals Designed to Upgrade Donors' Gifts*
- *Appeal Letter Uses Celebrity Signers Tied to Mission*
- *Pledge Fulfillment Rates*
- *Why Allow Credit Card Payments?*
- *Reach Into the Response Rate Tool Chest*
- *Make Gifts and Member Club Names Distinctive*
- *Three Ways to Increase Direct Mail Response Rates*
- *Add Spice to Your Pledge Billings*
- *Boost Your Appeal Response Rate*
- *Bounce Backs Increase Response Rate*

TABLE OF CONTENTS

Chapter 8:   **Examples From Which to Learn** 36

- *Monthly Letter Serves as Relationship-builder, Indirect Solicitation*
- *Direct Mail Tip*
- *Creative Solicitation Draws Donors*
- *Getting Away With Multiple Appeals to the Same Prospects*
- *Direct Mail Tips*
- *Personalized Message Makes for Direct Mail Appeal Success*
- *Recognize 'Lifetime Value' in Evaluating Results*
- *Direct Mail Idea*
- *Gift Asks Combine New Brochures, Personalized Solicitations*
- *Holiday Card Serves as Last-minute Appeal*
- *Long-time Organization's First Appeal a Success*
- *Postcard Encourages Giving for Honor Roll*
- *New Direct Mail Package Helps to Increase Number of Contributors*

Chapter 9:   **Evaluation Should Be Ongoing** 42

- *Analyze Direct Mail Renewal Methods*
- *Analyze Appeal to Improve Future Results*
- *Measure Your Direct Mail ROI*
- *Know Your Cost Per Response*
- *RFM Formula Measures Direct Mail Success*
- *Track Each Direct Mail Appeal's Success*
- *Direct Mail Tip*
- *Assess Direct Mail Contact Frequency*
- *It Pays to Conduct Direct Mail Cost Analysis*

Chapter 10:   **Planning Worksheet** 45

Profitable Direct Mail Appeals: Planning, Implementing and Maximizing Results, Second Edition.
Edited by Scott C. Stevenson.
© 2009 Stevenson, Inc. Published 2009 by Stevenson, Inc.

PLAN YOUR DIRECT MAIL YEAR

Far too many nonprofits use the "decide as we go" direct mail approach throughout their fiscal year. To make the most of gift revenue derived through direct mail, plan your entire year of appeals in advance: when they will be mailed, to whom, for what funding projects, what the contents of each package will be and what key messages will be conveyed. Also, set in place a system that will track results.

Keep Refining Your Yearlong Direct Mail Appeal Plan

It's wise to have a 12-month written plan outlining all direct mail appeals you'll send to particular groups throughout the upcoming year. It makes even more sense to refine that plan as you move from one year to another.

Create a calendar that identifies all planned appeals for the year, including those directed to past contributors and non-donors. (The example shown here includes personalized anniversary letters to those who gave during a particular month in the prior year.) Then, as you near the completion of the current year, formulate a new calendar for the subsequent year that includes revisions to the previous year's schedule.

This year-to-year comparison of direct mail appeals helps identify which segments of your database will be receiving particular invitations to support your organization.

Sunset Retirement Community: Yearlong Appeals Plan		
Drop Date	**2008 Appeals**	**2009 Appeals**
1/3	Anniversary Letter January '07 contributors	Anniversary Letter January '08 contributors
1/15	Non-donor Businesses (50-mile radius)	Non-donor Businesses (50-mile radius)
2/3	Anniversary Letter February '07 contributors	Anniversary Letter February '08 contributors
2/15		Special Memorial Appeal: Families of former residents
3/3	Anniversary Letter March '07 contributors	Anniversary Letter March '08 contributors
4/3	Anniversary Letter April '07 contributors	Anniversary Letter April '08 contributors
4/15	Non-donor local residents	Non-donor local residents
5/3	Anniversary Letter May '07 Contributors	Anniversary Letter May '08 Contributors
6/3	Anniversary Letter June '07 contributors	Anniversary Letter June '08 contributors
7/3	Anniversary Letter July '07 contributors	Anniversary Letter July '08 contributors
8/3	Anniversary Letter August '07 contributors	Anniversary Letter August '08 contributors
9/3	Anniversary Letter September '07 contributors	Anniversary Letter September '08 contributors
9/15		Special appeal: $250 prospects
10/3	Anniversary Letter October '07 contributors	Anniversary Letter October '08 contributors
11/3	Anniversary Letter November '07 contributors	Anniversary Letter November '08 contributors
11/10	General Appeal (entire list excluding current contributors)	General Appeal (entire list excluding current contributors)
12/3	Anniversary Letter November '07 contributors	Anniversary Letter November '08 contributors

PLAN YOUR DIRECT MAIL YEAR

Develop Your Entire Year's Direct Mail Plan

Whether your organization sends out direct mail solicitations yearly or monthly, you need a plan to stay on track. Consider this time line and checklist as an organizational tool:

Understand your goals before you begin. While direct mail is used to increase the number of new donors and upgrade past donors, it is not the way to raise major gifts.

Determine a budget for your program, taking into account the frequency of your mailings and the number of prospects you will solicit with each one.

Set a fundraising goal, but be realistic. Sometimes just breaking even on a mailing is good if it promises a payoff of increased donors over the years — lifetime value.

Establish a desired drop date and work backwards from that to set the time line for each part of the project. While most nonprofits send year-end solicitations in November or December, any time of year can be right for you depending on your circumstances. A mailing could work around an anniversary for your organization, holiday like Valentine's Day or Easter or other meaningful date. Consider staffing issues for all parts of the process so you have enough people to handle mailing and gift processing at the critical periods.

Create the letters and design the inserts. Determine a use for funds raised — either unrestricted or earmarked for a particular use.

Determine the letter's subject. If you're soliciting unrestricted dollars, pick a program or new technology to focus on and explain that it is just one of the many things the donors can help fund.

Find a story that establishes the need. This could be a challenge that has a successful outcome thanks to your organization, or an example of how the problem could not be solved because of a shortage of funding. For background and help in selecting the best story, conduct interviews with staff or those who have used your services, if necessary.

Draft, edit and revise the letter. Have several staff members and even outside parties give you feedback on errors and tone. Draft acknowledgment letters at the same time so you're prepared when the first donations arrive.

Collect signatures, logos and pictures, in either hard-copy or electronic format. Decide who is the appropriate person to make the case by signing the letter and what pictures best tell the story.

Lay out the reply cards and any other inserts, including text and pictures to tie in with those used in the letter, tracking codes for analyzing the responses, and appropriate ask amounts.

Collect and segment lists. Select your audience from your database. Decide if you'll include major gift prospects, board members, memorial donors, etc. Eliminate those with incorrect addresses or who have requested no direct mail solicitation. Obtain mailing lists from others within your organization if needed, such as schools, departments, patient records, etc.

Purchase lists from outside vendors. Work with your vendor to determine the best lists for your market and budget. Note that rented lists come with specific time frames that will require you to stick to your established drop date.

Plan to segment your mailing? Determine ask amounts for the various groups. Make sure your reply cards and letters match the segmented amounts.

Have duplicates removed from lists or discuss having your mail house "de-dup" them before letters are generated. Establish a hierarchy for address and ask amount selections.

Process your lists through national change of address (NCOA) services, if necessary. You may also put postal return information on your outside envelopes.

Work with your printer and post office. Print letterhead, envelopes, reply cards, inserts and business reply envelopes, allowing for a sufficient overage amount. Make sure your nonprofit business mail permit is paid, enough money is deposited in your postal account for mail returns and business reply envelope (BRE) costs, and you have stamps or a check for the mail house to cover postage on the letters.

Coordinate plans with your mail house. Give advance notice of the mailing so they can fit it into their time line and inform you of any requirements (especially important for mailings in November/December or that are complex or extremely large).

Provide written instructions and talk to your representative about all your expectations and requirements. Have the rep sign off on your request and give you a written estimate in advance, especially if you've never used that mail house before.

Deliver the letter text, signatures, pictures and mailing lists, in hard-copy or electronic format, as required. Have the printer deliver stationery, reply cards and inserts. Get samples and overages on supplies returned to you.

After the mailing, process the donations using tracking codes to segment responses. Make database corrections for addresses and names as needed. Acknowledge the gifts as you receive them. Include gift club premiums as needed.

Analyze the donations by segment and for overall results, and determine what was most effective and what needs to be changed for the next mailing.

Direct Mail Tip

How long should an appeal letter be? Although answers will vary, here's one tip to keep in mind: Likely donors are more willing to read long letters. Nondonors won't, so keep it to one page (or less) for the latter group.

PLAN YOUR DIRECT MAIL YEAR

Evaluating Direct Mail Consultants

Hiring a direct mail consultant? Look for quality writing, says Jim Moore, general partner with CommUlinks of Colorado (Aurora, CO).

"Look at samples and ask to talk to the script writer," Moore says. "Get a sense of the writer's understanding of your mission. Is he or she a student of nonprofit missions? Is he or she a fountain of ideas — perhaps a bit off base without your guidance, but obviously inspired and in tune with your message? Can he or she articulate a well-crafted formula for developing an effective message? "Does the company have data to back up its opinions about message strategy?"

When evaluating direct mail consultants, says Moore, also consider:

- **The company's access to lists, as well as its members' skills regarding research, negotiation and management.** Can the company get you access to good lists for trades and/or at good rates? More importantly, does the staff understand the best synergies between other organizations and yours?

- **How well they understand your constituents' demographics.** Are they going to suggest tactics that fit your constituents or are they going to push one-size-fits-all concepts on mail packaging and messages?

- **Data analysis quality.** How well will the company analyze your mailings' performance? Does staff provide a meticulous breakdown by mail package, list, letter type, color/black-and-white, etc.? They should produce lots of data, including long-term analysis of return-on-investment from each donor/member group based on every imaginable parameter. They should discover useful trends or factors in your data that are not obvious without this analysis.

- **Number of clients they have had with missions similar to yours.** Obviously, you don't want a conflict of interest, but a company that has worked exclusively for museums, historic preservation or arts/cultural groups may face a steep learning curve for its first few human services clients. A company whose greatest successes are on behalf of advocacy organizations might not be the best choice for a religious group.

- **How they set their rates.** What is the unit price on mail packages similar to those you might send? The consultant's fee is just the tip of the iceberg on costs. Direct mail consultants rely heavily on relationships with other vendors — bonded mail houses, printers, list sellers, paper suppliers, warehouse operators, etc. Will they itemize invoices? Financial Accounting Standards Board (FASB) cost allocation is far easier and more credible if you get a breakdown of costs: consulting, printing, lists rental, bonded mail house mail handling and merge costs, etc.

- **How they allocate other costs.** Fundraising messages are often actually a combination of two or three expense streams: fundraising; public education and sometimes legislative advocacy (lobbying). How well does the consulting firm understand these accounting issues, and how clearly can its staff craft a message and mail package that makes it easy to accurately allocate mailing expenses along these expense lines? How defensible is your position going to be if audited?

Source: Jim Moore, General Partner, CommUlinks of Colorado, Aurora, CO. Phone: (303) 400-3456. E-mail:jim@commulinks.com

Create a System For Coding Appeals

One way that US Lacrosse (Baltimore, MD) tracks its mailed appeals is by including a coordinated online appeal with every solicitation, says Valerie Lambert, associate director of financial development. "We do this whether it's through our magazine, on the buckslip or envelope of a direct mail piece, during phonathon, or simply when we send an acknowledgment to a donor and enclose a return envelope for their 'next donation,'" she says.

Each of these appeals has a distinctive hyperlink, says Lambert, which is different from the "Donate Now" button on the organization's website. "Surfing our website will only take you to the 'Donate Now' page," she says. "The donor MUST manually type in the hyperlink from the appeal so we know that they are at this donation page because they are responding to the specific appeal."

When a donor goes to one of these links, says Lambert, they will see the same page, however: "It displays the same text, same photo as on our direct mail piece, updated with each new drop."

They have three 'codes' for each appeal code, she says. For example, when they had a spring mailing for 2006, their appeal coding read: SP 2006 phone; SP 2006 USPS; SP 2006 Web. More than 90 percent of gifts arrive through the mail, however Lambert says they are seeing more of an online donation presence and a few people still calling with a credit card gift.

Source: Valerie Lambert, Associate Director of Financial Development, US Lacrosse, Baltimore, MD. Phone (410) 235-6882, ext. 127. E-mail: vlambert@uslacrosse.org

PLAN YOUR DIRECT MAIL YEAR

Keep Direct Mail Pieces Simple, User-friendly

Planning a direct mail solicitation campaign takes more thought, budgeting and creativity now than ever before, partly because your potential donors and your loyal supporters have mailboxes already full to overflowing. And any piece that isn't simple, attractive — and, above all, user-friendly — is likely to go straight into the round file.

The costs of paper, printing and postage continue to rise. Your organization can help make every campaign mailing count by following some practical guidelines before launching into the design and printing stages:

❑ **Check with your local post office** to obtain a copy of the latest size and print placement elements to be sure regulations haven't changed since your last mailing. This could save you from having the post office hold return envelopes that contain checks because of unintentional noncompliance.

❑ **Keep the pieces of your mailing standard sized,** and be sure that each part of the mailing has a function — a simple brochure to explain your purpose and how funds will be used, a pledge card, and a pre-addressed return envelope are essential. A detachable pledge card could be combined with the brochure or return envelope, saving expenses.

❑ **Give credit to printers or sponsors** who have helped pay for costs associated with your direct mail appeal. If an in-kind donation has allowed you to send a more attractive piece that may give the impression unnecessary funds were spent for solicitation, thank the company with a brief notation on the piece. But ask them first if they'd like to be publicly thanked, because some in-kind donors prefer not to be noted.

❑ **Ask the donor for a stamp.**

Instead of postage-paid envelopes, note in the upper right-hand corner, "your stamp allows us to spend more to fulfill our mission."

❑ **Personalize addresses and salutations to the fullest extent.** If including a letter from your director or spokesman, try to use the donor's name. A "dear friend" greeting or computer-generated address tells the donor no one will notice if he/she doesn't respond because no one in the organization had specific hands-on involvement in the request.

❑ **Keep copy brief and informative.** Try highlighting the most important points in larger type with a color, or on a reverse background. Use bullet-point summaries of how funds will be used. Too much gray type or pages of copy cause most donors to set the mailing aside to read later.

❑ **Include an occasional small but useful gift.** Donors may enjoy receiving a token of thanks if it has a purpose — a refrigerator magnet with a one-year calendar and your phone number, a wallet card with a tipping guide and your mission, or half a dozen postcards featuring photos of activities you sponsor that the donor can really use (and spread your message) are examples. Donors may see gimmicky items with your logo as wasteful, but they may keep or carry practical items for years.

When you design or produce direct mail pieces, keep in mind solicitations you have received and recall how effective they were — did you send a check? Did they make it easy for you to respond in one or two steps? Did a photo or quote strike a chord with your generous, sympathetic side? Make use of some of the same concepts that moved you to send a gift and tailor them to your organization's needs.

How to Make Direct Mailings More Personal

They all look the same — a No. 10 envelope with a computer-generated name label and an appealing photograph. You don't need to open it to know it's an appeal for a gift.

When sending large campaign mailings to thousands who have had an interest in your institution, the little things mean a lot. Use some personal touches so the recipient knows someone was thinking specifically of him or her:

- Use a stamp.
- Hand write an attention line in pen on the envelope.
- Put a self-stick note with a brief hello on the brochure or write on a blank space.
- Sign each letter in a different color ink than the letter text.
- Ask volunteers to write short notes to key donors to enclose in the mailing, such as "Dave, thanks for all your help," and sign their own names.
- Refer in your letter to a specific instance or event that the potential donor knows about or attended. "It was gratifying to learn of your participation in our golf tournament." Be sure the personalization fits a targeted, but sizable, group of individuals.
- Choose an unusual style of envelope and paper stock.
- Hand address each envelope.
- Name both persons if mailing to a couple. Doing so instantly shows you recognize who they are.
- Mention in your letter a shared history with a large constituency when you can, and link it to your current topic. Choose an event that many will remember, but each in his or her personal way.

PLAN YOUR DIRECT MAIL YEAR

Managing Track Codes on Mailed Appeals

Q. *"Our organization codes reply envelopes to help us track to which appeal a donor is responding. We recently received envelopes coded for appeals as old as 2003, which means our donors are saving old reply envelopes and using them to make current donations. Should we credit those donations to the old appeals, or to the current years? How can we prevent this from happening in the first place?"*

Kevin D. Feldman, director of marketing communications, WorldVenture (formerly CBInternational) in Rockville, MD, suggests that rather than coding reply envelopes, code the response device: "That way if a donor saves envelopes to use at a later date, which many do, the envelope will be generic and the donation (unless otherwise noted on the check or on an included response device) can be used for the general fund.

"If you print the fund codes on the response device, you can more accurately determine what motivated the gift and where it should be designated."

Donors don't know what the appeal or fund codes mean, Feldman says. So when they save envelopes and give later, it is likely that something else other than that old appeal motivated them to give.

"For now, I would use this opportunity to personally contact those who have used envelopes from old appeals to make recent gifts," says Feldman. "Thank them, of course, and then ask them if your organization can use the money where it is needed most, or if they wanted their donation to be used in a particular way."

Christine L. Manor, an accounting consultant to nonprofit organizations and author of Quickbooks for Not-

for-Profit Organizations, says that for accounting purposes, those old appeals (before the current fiscal year) are no longer active.

"Even if you code a donation to the 2004 appeal, it will be recorded as a 2006 gift because you can't go back and restate the 2004 reports," she says. "Assuming that you are on a fiscal year other than a calendar year, a gift in January 2006 can (and should) be coded to the December 2005 appeal. If you are on a calendar year basis and the check is dated (and the envelope postmarked) in December, then you can consider the gift as 'constructively' received and record it as a receivable (and income) for December."

Sources: Christine L. Manor, Accounting Consultant to Not-for-Profit Organizations, Rockville, MD. Phone (301) 762-7798. E-mail: clm@clmanor.com
Kevin D. Feldman, Director of Marketing Communications, WorldVenture, Littleton, CO. Phone (720) 283-2000.

Shrewd Direct Mail Planning

Rather than whipping together a direct mail appeal and getting it out the door at the last minute, put some thought into your entire year of appeals.

For example:

- Before sending a direct mail appeal, write a brief marketing plan to set its direction. This marketing plan should cover target audience, audience demographics, quantity, key message(s), appeal package composition, funding project(s), estimated cost, anticipated revenue and other key factors.

- Plan a series of appeals rather than assuming a onetime request will meet your goal.

Use Appeal Codes to Track Gifts

Coding envelopes or response devices is a great idea if, as a practitioner, you want to know what it is that may be motivating your donor to participate or give, says Susan D. Smith, a philanthropy consultant in Barneveld, New York.

Codes can be useful tracking tools, Smith says, particularly if you use them to determine how an individual came to be among your donors; but be careful about using coded envelopes and pledge cards to gauge when someone has decided to become involved.

"For whatever reason — environmental responsibility, not wanting to waste a perfectly good envelope, being able to find a mailer for your organization when the spirit to make a gift hits — many donors do save envelopes, pledge cards, 'In Honor of' and 'In Memory of'

gift forms, regardless of when they are received, or of their original purpose in a mailing," says Smith.

At a nonprofit where Smith worked several years ago, she says, she designed a direct mail piece to purposely be quite different from one the organization had used for 20-plus years. Although they used the new piece for several mailings during her tenure, she says, many donors used envelopes from 10, 15, sometimes 20 years before. "Though they hadn't given to those campaigns in years past (a check of the donor histories confirmed that), they had saved every envelope!"

Source: Susan D. Smith, Consultant in Philanthropy, Barneveld, NY. Phone (315) 896-8524. E-mail: sdsmith@ntcnet.com

Profitable Direct Mail Appeals: Planning, Implementing and Maximizing Results, Second Edition.
Edited by Scott C. Stevenson.
© 2009 Stevenson, Inc. Published 2009 by Stevenson, Inc.

LISTS AND LIST MANAGEMENT

Your mailing list is the most priceless component of your direct mail apparatus. Those persons and businesses on your mailing list provide the ultimate source of gift potential you hope to realize. That's why ongoing attention should be given to selectively expanding, deliberately pruning and meticulously managing your list of donors and would-be donors.

Spend Time Developing Your Mailing List

If your organization has little fundraising history, begin by developing a solid mailing list or database to solicit funds through direct mail appeals, personal calls and telesolicitation. List persons with current or past connection to your organization, such as:

- Clients/customers (e.g., past/present students, patients, members, attendees)

- Anyone who ever made a gift to your organization

- Volunteers; current/past employees; board members

- Local businesses (begin with chamber members)

- Other local nonprofit organizations

- Residents in ZIP codes around your service area

With the database in place, start strategizing ways to approach potential supporters.

Database Info

While you will eventually add more background information (e.g., linkage to charity, financial information, etc.), your initial mailing list should include these basic components:

- ✓ Prospect name
- ✓ Title
- ✓ Spouse
- ✓ Home address and phone
- ✓ Business address and phone
- ✓ E-mail addresses

Building a Mailing List From Scratch Or Build on an Existing One

Whether expanding an established mailing list or starting from scratch, it's important to selectively build your list if you hope to cultivate new and larger gifts. Begin by adding names of those persons who already contribute to or make use of your organization's services.

Here are some ways to capture names with giving potential:

1. Place a guest book in key locations frequented by visitors.

2. Have a fish bowl available for business cards — include a monthly drawing for a donated item.

3. Include a return postcard in mailings inviting new names to be added to your mailing list.

4. Add all current, past and potential vendors.

5. Review names of top donors to other organizations and add their names to your list.

6. Include current as well as past board members.

7. Include current and retired employees.

8. Don't forget the obvious: Those who have benefited from your services and perhaps relatives of former clients (e.g., students, patients, members).

9. Include active and past volunteers.

10. Selectively add residents of exclusive ZIP/postal codes.

11. Expand your list of major businesses and foundations.

Gather E-mail Addresses

Have you been collecting e-mail addresses of those on your regular mailing list? E-mail can be another means of cultivating constituents and provide another avenue for soliciting support. Another important benefit: No postage fees!

Collect the addresses by:

1. Sending a postcard to your entire mailing list inviting everyone to "send, fax, call or e-mail your e-mail addresses back to us."

2. Including a place for e-mail addresses on all pledge forms and other bounce backs.

3. When conducting phonathons, instruct callers to ask for e-mail addresses at the end of the call, when verifying the donor's address.

Build a Mailing List Of Qualified Names

If you have a mailing list of 1,000 quality names and get a 3 percent response rate, it makes sense to build your list — with quality names — even if the response rate drops somewhat.

One cost-effective alternative to building a donor base is to get names from board members, volunteers and current donors and send out personalized letters. Each board member, volunteer and donor could write a personal note on the letters that are being sent to people he/she knows. This procedure accomplishes another worthwhile objective as well: It gets your constituents involved in fund development, and their increased involvement may lead to increased giving.

LISTS AND LIST MANAGEMENT

Turn to Those You Serve for Names

Want to build your mailing list? Turn to those you serve: students, graduates, former patients, members and others.

Invite those you serve, as well as those you have served in the past, to share the names of family, friends and associates with your organization.

To encourage them to add to your mailing list:

- **Invite referrals through direct mail.** Include bounce backs in all of your mailings. Send a special appeal that asks for a gift and names of potential donors. Include a P.S. on individual correspondence and e-mails.

- **Ask online.** Use your website to invite visitors to submit names to be added to your mailing list.

- **Take advantage of public gatherings.** Whenever you have an event, ask those present to fill out a referral card or share referral names with a staff person.

- **Don't overlook the use of premiums.** Consider offering inexpensive premiums to anyone who refers names: a free ticket to an event, discount coupons and more.

- **Ask for names during one-on-one meetings.** Whenever you call on a current contributor, don't leave without asking for a referral.

Call Reports Are More Than a Record

If you're new to development, a call report is a written summary of what was said during a meeting with a prospect or donor. A call report should always be completed following substantive communication with a prospect or donor. Persons who think the purpose behind a call report is simply to provide a record of what was said, however, are wrong. Although call reports do leave a lasting record of key conversation points, they should also accomplish other key aims. The completed call report should:

1. **Point out the primary objective of the call.** Was the visit intended to cultivate a prospect, solicit the prospect, introduce your organization to someone new or perhaps learn more about a prospect's funding interests? This key objective should be known prior to the visit and should be recorded as the first item on the call report.

2. **Illustrate the degree to which the caller accomplished the stated objective.** The summary of the visit should provide answers as to whether the objective was met.

3. **Make mention of next steps.** Follow-up is crucial to any prospect/donor communication. It's important to articulate follow-up steps after all key communications and include the time frame in which those steps should be completed (e.g., solicit gift within two weeks, deliver a proposal in 30 days, etc.).

Update Lost Addresses

Part of good database management is keeping addresses as current as possible. But that's sometimes easier said than done with the mobility of today's society.

To help retrieve updated addresses for lost constituents:

- ❑ List lost constituents' names on your website with a link to an e-mail to send current contact information should the person being sought or someone who knows where he/she is reads it.

- ❑ Include lists of lost constituents in particular mailings, including an e-mail or toll-free number to contact with current information.

- ❑ Display names of lost constituents at your events along with a "Help us find these important folks!" note.

- ❑ Check with constituents' last known employers. If they won't share a current address, ask them to forward mail that asks for updated addresses.

CALL REPORT — XYZ CHARITY

Name of Prospect/Donor _____

Call Made By _____ Date of Call _____

Type of Call (Phone, personal visit, etc.) _____ Location _____

Primary Objective: _____

Summary of Call: _____

_____

_____

Next Steps/Deadline

1. _____

2. _____

3. _____

LISTS AND LIST MANAGEMENT

Use Tracer Cards to Locate Lost Constituents

Keeping track of constituents is an important task of any fundraising organization. If you don't know where they are, you can't keep them informed about programs and can't solicit them for funds.

Tracer cards such as the one shown below are one method for locating lost constituents. If you are unable to locate a constituent, send the tracer cards to his/her relatives or last known employers. Or mail them to constituents to verify new addresses when you first learn of them.

In addition to making sure a home address is correct, ask the constituent for a new phone number, business address, e-mail address and other pertinent information. The cards are also appropriate to send to newly married or newly employed constituents, asking for updated names and addresses while also offering congratulations.

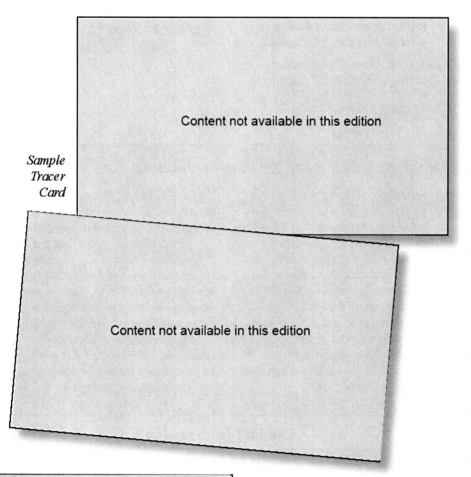

Sample Tracer Card

Content not available in this edition

Content not available in this edition

Content not available in this edition

Build Your E-mail Database

E-mail has opened up an entirely new avenue of communication to use to introduce, cultivate, solicit and steward. Work to build your e-mail database at every touch point you have with prospects and donors: pledge forms, sign-up sheets, change-of-address forms, etc.

How Do You Define Your Solicitable Base?

What your solicitable base is depends on whether you define it as who is solicitable or who you decide to solicit, says Sarah Berger, annual fund director, The College of St. Catherine (St. Paul, MN).

Who is solicitable and who you decide to solicit are two different things, she says: "I believe you get into tricky territory if you eliminate those prospects who have not given for three years in order to increase your participation rate. It's different if you consider them solicitable but choose not to spend money soliciting them."

Berger says they solicit everyone. "It's amazing how long someone can be lapsed or be a non-donor and appear out of nowhere — often because life circumstances change or the college did something that made them proud so they show it with a contribution."

Think twice before excluding certain donors/prospects from your database because they haven't given in a few years, she says.

If you're experiencing poor response rates, ask yourself:

- Do we have good contact information for our prospects?
- How many times do we contact prospects before they make a gift? Berger says four to six contacts is ideal.
- Is the poor response rate new? Has something changed?
- Are we segmenting and personalizing enough?
- If we eliminate donors who haven't given for three years, what will be the long-term impact of that decision?

Source: Sarah Berger, Director of the Annual Fund, The College of St. Catherine, St. Paul, MN. Phone (651) 690-8840. E-mail: slberger@stkate.edu

LISTS AND LIST MANAGEMENT

How to Build a Database of Qualified Prospects

The first question fundraisers need to ask when starting the process of building a database of qualified prospects is: Who cares about us and why?

"If an organization's mission statement is truly in sync with what the organization is doing, it provides a way to help identify who cares about it and why," says Tony Poderis, consultant.

Whether they are stewards of other people's money or individual contributors, people who are willing to give to an organization usually fall into one of two groups, says Poderis: those whose lives have been touched by the organization or those who are influenced and impressed by an organization's work or its leadership.

"Hospitals always put former patients high on their list of potential donors because their lives have been touched by the organization," he says. "Schools have entire departments devoted to alumni relations."

Every organization should have a database of its clients/users to prospect for donors, says Poderis, because even if the organization serves a clientele unlikely to be able to make gifts, those clients may lead to previously untapped sources. "When I worked for Big Brothers of Cleveland, which served more than 500 boys who did not have fathers at home, the mothers weren't able to give much money but a little research showed 10 percent of them worked at a utility company. When we pointed this out in our solicitation of the utility company and included endorsements from employees/mothers, we received gifts in excess of the company's usual. So, when it comes to finding donors: prospect, prospect, prospect and look for connections."

Poderis says viable prospects can be found by:

- Asking for names from your organization's board of trustees; suggestions from those already giving; and suggestions of new prospects from participants in prospect identification and rating

meetings who know the community and have money to give.
- Searching public resources (e.g., library, business publication, etc.), which have records of stock ownership, real estate holdings, salary data, business and career histories, family tree information, etc. of those with the means and history of giving money and who live and work in your service area.
- Gathering annual reports from similar organizations and reviewing their donor listings as potential donors to your cause.

Source: Tony Poderis, Consultant and Author, Willoughby Hills, OH. Phone (440) 944-9230. E-mail: tony@raise-funds.com

Records Management Tip

Trying to determine if someone in your database has passed away? You will find any of these sites to be helpful:

www.legacy.com — Nationwide resource for obituaries.

www.ancestry.com — Family history records on the Internet.

www.rootsweb.com — Free genealogy website.

Maintain a Summary Sheet in Each Donor File

How many times have you gone to a prospect's or donor's file seeking one piece of information and having to look through the entire file to locate it?

While many nonprofits have sophisticated computer software to record donor information, there will always be a place for the traditional filing system as a way of maintaining information that 1) may be too cumbersome for computer records, and, 2) serves as an important backup in the event of a computer crash.

To help reduce file review time, attach a contact information sheet inside the cover of each prospect/donor file.

All too often important data is lost because there's no easy way to capture it, or staff turns over and it's gone forever. The contact sheet provides an easy way to summarize visits and correspondence with prospects over a period of time.

Summary sheets can also keep a running total of gifts made along with the purpose of each gift and a corresponding gift acknowledgment date.

Contact Information

CONTACT NAME/ADDRESS		PHONE/FAX
DATE	ACTION	

Profitable Direct Mail Appeals: Planning, Implementing and Maximizing Results, Second Edition.
Edited by Scott C. Stevenson.
© 2009 Stevenson, Inc. Published 2009 by Stevenson, Inc.

SEGMENT AND TARGET KEY AUDIENCES

Those organizations that realize the highest returns are those that have refined their ability to segment their mailing list into various groups and target each with appropriate appeals — nondonors as opposed to past donors, past donors at varying giving levels, affinity groups, prospects based on age or gender or geographic location.

Mail, E-mail Solicitations Target Young Alumni Donors

The University of North Carolina recently sent a direct mail appeal to 13,824 young alumni lapsed donors as a way to encourage young alumni giving and to drive traffic to its young alumni giving website.

The target group included those who had made an annual gift in one of the last five years, but not last year, and those who made a past gift, but not in the last five years.

"The purpose of the mailing was to prime young alumni for other solicitations and phonathon calls," says Malaika Marie Underwood, director of young alumni. "No gift slip was included with the mailing, which in retrospect we would change so that we could track the direct gift impact of the piece. We did, however, code those people who received the mailing. It was sent in March, and 871 people have responded with a gift."

They followed up the direct mail piece with an e-mail solicitation — http://carolinafirst.unc.edu/youngalumni/email/youngalumni/youngalumni.htm — a few weeks later, Underwood says. "The e-mail piece provided recipients of the direct mail piece with a convenient reminder and informed young alumni who didn't receive the direct mail piece about how they can help Carolina. It included a direct link to our website for more information and encouraged them to make a gift." The follow-up e-mail was sent to the 26,833 young alumni for whom they had an e-mail

address; 7,492 of those were opened.

Plans include a second e-mail solicitation to young alums who haven't given this fiscal year. The e-mail will highlight two donors, one who has given consistently, and one who gave for the first time this year, to play off the university's young alumni theme: "Every gift makes a difference…especially yours."

As a result of these efforts, website traffic has increased dramatically, Underwood says. "In the last six months, page views on our young alumni website have increased by 500 percent. Compared to last year, we are up 21 percent in young alumni dollars and we are improving donor numbers. We are reversing what was a negative trend; we are only down 4 percent in young alumni donors. There is also a lot of momentum building — we are definitely making headway in educating young alumni about giving."

Source: Malaika Marie Underwood, Director of Young Alumni, University of North Carolina, Chapel Hill, NC. Phone (919) 260-3521. E-mail: underwood@unc.edu

Messages to Persuade Lapsed Donors

Do you direct targeted appeals to lapsed donors designed to get them back on board?

To help you create the most suitable message for your audience, here are some phrases you may wish to consider:

- Your support continues to mean so much to us. May we count on you again this year?

- We've missed your participation. Please join us for another year.

- I don't know any other way to say it: If your support isn't there this year, we won't be able to....

- We take great pride in having your name associated with our agency. I hope we can count on your participation again this year.

- I was reviewing our list of contributors to date and noticed your name was missing. That's why I wanted to contact you and share this friendly reminder.

- There's a good chance we will break a new record in gift support this year, but only if past contributors continue to invest generously in our effort. Can we count on you for a gift of....?

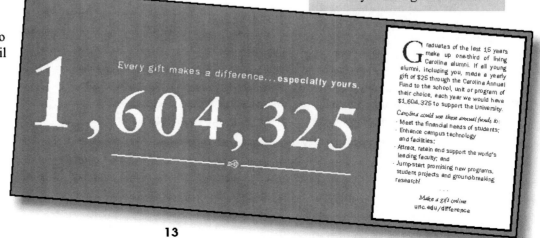

SEGMENT AND TARGET KEY AUDIENCES

Anniversary Letters
Offer Effective Way of Renewing Support

When it comes to renewing annual contributions through direct mail, here's a tried-and-true method: sending personalized letters to donors on the anniversary of their previous year's gift. This technique — with letters generally sent monthly — spreads the work load and ensures a continuous flow of gift revenue throughout the year.

If anniversary letters could be the best way for you to renew annual gifts, here are some ideas you could incorporate:

- **Include timely information.** If you're sending a group of renewal letters monthly, include a paragraph or two of up-to-date news about your organization to keep the message timely and interesting in the eyes of the reader. In fact, use a current piece of news to justify why you need increased support: "Susan, if you could increase this year's gift to $200, it would help us more fully address the overcrowding problem now facing us."

- **Compare last year's support to this year's request.** Point out the dollar amount that the donor gave in the previous fiscal year and ask for a specific dollar increase for a specific purpose: "Tom, we are grateful that you contributed $75 to last year's effort. This year we ask that you consider a gift of $125 to enable us to cover camp fees for one additional (and deserving) student."

- **Thank them in advance.** Enclose complimentary tickets to an upcoming event in advance of the donor's gift as a gesture of kindness and confidence in his/her commitment to your cause.

- **Update them on status of gifts to date.** If it's to your advantage, share the status of overall annual gifts to date and what needs to happen to surpass your annual fund goal.

Once your monthly anniversary renewal program is in place, keep enhancing it (e.g., producing various follow-up letters for those who did not respond to your first request). Try it for six months to determine if this method works well for your organization.

Turn Sybunts Into Consistent Supporters

Looking for a way to re-involve past donors? Conduct a sybunt campaign.

Scott Davis, fund development coordinator, Hope House of Milwaukee (Milwaukee, WI), says this is useful in two ways: 1) if they respond with support, that's a re-established relationship or 2) if they don't respond, then they are removed from the mailing list, which saves money.

"We go back in our records two years and send an appeal letter to re-visit and re-invest in Hope House," says Davis. "In the letter I explain what we've done recently and invite the donor to come back."

For their 2006 sybunt campaign, Davis and staff reviewed their database and found 761 people who last gave in 2003 or 2004. "We reviewed these donors and pared our list down to about 250 — we only sent letters to donors who gave more than $25," says Davis. The result: $1,643. However, since that mailing those donors have given an additional $3,517. "This really paid in spades for us because we received 50 times what we needed to break even," he says.

From the 2006 results, they will be cutting approximately 500 donors from their mailing list. "After cutting those names, that's $400 in savings that can be used to focus on donors and give them more attention," he says.

Source: Scott Davis, Fund Development Coordinator, Hope House of Milwaukee, Milwaukee, WI. Phone (414) 389-3845. E-mail: scottd@hope-house.com

Segment Past Donors According to Gift Clubs

To move donors to the next gift club up on your rung, consider doing a separate direct mail appeal to each giving group.

If, for example, you have a gift club for those who gave $100 to $249 last year, and want to upgrade them to the next level that starts at $250, send those persons an appeal letter inviting them to join the $250 club. Take the same approach with each gift club, pointing out benefits associated with stepping up to the next giving level. Include in the direct mail package a brochure pointing out benefits associated with that next higher gift club.

(This is where having exclusive benefits for each gift club can really pay off.)

You may even want letters to be signed by one or two individuals who are members of the gift club you are seeking to have your donors join.

SEGMENT AND TARGET KEY AUDIENCES

Tailor Brochures to Targeted Age Groups

Finding it difficult to appeal to different age groups in one direct mail appeal? Why not do what officials with Agnes Scott College (Decatur, GA) did with their annual fund mailings?

Agnes Scott's annual fund brochures, which won a CASE (Council for Advancement and Support of Education) award, were targeted to specific groups of alumnae.

"At an annual fund staff meeting, we were talking about how difficult it is to write a letter which appeals to all age groups," says Joanne Davis, director of annual fund. "We discussed how far apart in ages our alumnae are, from in their 90s to their early 20s, and wondered if there wasn't something different we could do to connect with them and catch their attention."

The brainstorming phase of the project involved gaining perspectives from several people — alumnae director (a 1968 alumna), creative services director, freelance designer, annual fund officer (a 2003 alumna), two associate annual fund directors and Davis.

"After much discussion, we decided it would be a good idea to divide and conquer," says Davis. "In other words, divide our constituency into groups by decades and do four brochures for alumnae and one for current parents and parents of alumnae." The groups were older alumnae ('25 to '59), alumnae ('60s to '79), alumnae ('80 to '92), young alumnae ('93 to '03) and current students' parents and parents of graduates.

Each mailer included a photo montage featuring an age-appropriate alumna with nostalgic photos from her era and the theme, "The Power of One — The Impact of Many."

"We thought they might pay more attention

"We wanted something that would catch their attention immediately and make them think about the college and the part it played in their life."

to a piece that contained few words but had pictures that would evoke nostalgia and make them understand every gift is important and every gift, large or small, makes a difference," says Davis. "We wanted something that would catch their attention immediately and make them think about the college and the part it played in their life."

The college got a lot of mileage out of the brochures' theme. An e-solicitation with music and some of the same photos was a big hit, says Davis, but unfortunately, they weren't able to track results. The brochures brought in about $30,000 that they were able to track.

The images on the front of the brochures were used to make four postcards for fund chairs to write thank-you notes. Final appeal postcards and year-end, thank-you postcards were also created.

Source: Joanne A. Davis, Director of Annual Fund, Office of Development, Agnes Scott College, Decatur, GA. Phone (404) 471-5343. E-mail: jadavis@ agnesscott.edu

Test Appeals To Non-donors

Unsure about the best way to turn non-donors into first-time contributors? Why not test two direct mail appeals?

Try this:

1. Send one mailing to half of your non-donors that includes a wish list of specific funding projects with varying price tags.

2. Send another appeal to the remaining half asking for general support to underwrite the work of your organization (no specific projects).

Chances are the wish list appeal will produce better results. People like knowing exactly how their gifts are being used and that they are making a difference. But by testing two appeals, you will learn what works best for you.

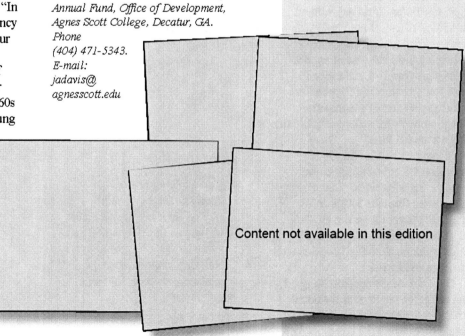

Content not available in this edition

SEGMENT AND TARGET KEY AUDIENCES

Generational Segmenting Boosts Response Rate

It was music to the ears of supporters of Manchester College (North Manchester, IN).

Staff at the liberal arts college took a clever approach to generational segmenting by using song titles and experienced a 3 percent increase in its response rate.

Janeen Kooi, director, The Manchester Fund, segmented more than 7,100 lybunt (gave last year but not this) and sybunt (gave some years but not this) alumni, parents and friends into five groups. Each group received a greeting card with a generationally appropriate song title, photo and corresponding tagline.

"Although all received the same message about the needs of the college, the tagline and the greeting message were segmented to match the song title," Kooi says.

"The song title was chosen to elicit an emotional response and to motivate action. For instance, research shows that 'civics' (those of the World War II era) respond to duty, responsibility and helping the next generation. So, the message was to 'Let the Good Times Roll,' as they did for you, for another generation of Manchester College students by making a gift to the college's annual fund."

In addition to "Let the Good Times Roll," Kooi carefully chose the following song titles: "Stand by Me" (alumni from the 1950s-'60s), "Imagine" (alumni from the 1970s) and "You Are the Wind Beneath My Wings" (alumni from the 1980s, as well as parents and friends).

Once she determined the song title, Kooi wrote the tag lines and worked with the college's archivist to find photos representing the corresponding

An appeal for The Manchester Fund for Manchester College (North Manchester, IN) features greeting cards designed with specific constituent groups in mind. This is the card used for alumni from the 1950s and '60s.

time period. Parents and friends received a photo of recent and current students with a current professor.

While a complete data analysis is yet to occur, Kooi says the pictures, song titles and messages resonated with the donors.

Source: Janeen Kooi, Director of The Manchester Fund, Manchester College, North Manchester, IN.
Phone (260) 982-5202.
E-mail: jwkooi@manchester.edu

List Management Tip

■ Do all of your printed materials ask for e-mail addresses? If not, be sure and add such a line. E-mail offers a fast-growing medium for notifying, cultivating and, in some instances, soliciting constituents.

Analyze Your Mailing List at Least Annually

When was the last time you reviewed your database to determine who is and is not contributing on an annual basis?

Should your list be expanded or pruned? Do you have solicitation strategies aimed at specific list segments?

Analyzing your list and developing strategies aimed at increasing the overall percentage of annual contributors is well worth the time and effort involved.

To fine-tune your mailing list, conduct these exercises:

- Determine the existing percentage of those who contributed last year and set a challenging percentage increase as next year's goal.

- Identify your list's lybunts (those who gave last year but not this) and sybunts (those who give some years but not this) and develop strategies to secure their gifts.

- Evaluate the demographics of your non-donors (age, gender, location and more) to determine targeted strategies. For example, you may want to solicit prospects geographically for projects that will benefit their communities or regions.

- Evaluate your system of donor benefits and incentives. Should changes be made?

- Share your list of non-donors with board members, your development committee or other key volunteers, and develop a plan that encourages them to help solicit particular persons or businesses.

SEGMENT AND TARGET KEY AUDIENCES

Postcards Educate Students On Importance of Philanthropy

What is your development office's position on cultivating young people as donors?

If you don't currently have a policy in place to reach out to young adults, consider creating one. After all, it's never too early to nurture philanthropy.

Officials with the University of South Carolina (Columbia, SC) realized the captive audience of future donors they had in their students, and decided that it wasn't too soon to begin forming relationships with their future prospects.

Steve Farwick, assistant director of annual giving, says the university is two years into using student philanthropy education postcards (shown below) to get the message out about the impact alumni giving plays in their education.

"We want students to realize that alumni are helping them while they are pursuing their degrees. Many students think their tuition is enough to operate the entire university," says Farwick. "By educating students early, they will have a better sense of philanthropy and will understand what it is all about. If they are informed as students, they will more likely want to give when they become alumni."

Each 6 X 9-inch postcard is one in a series of three designed internally by the university's publications office. Farwick says the focus of the postcard's design was his office's student philanthropy theme, "Students Today, Alumni Forever."

The front of the postcard features a picture of a student/young alumnus looking up at different words. On the left half under the headline, "Students Today," are words students currently think about (e.g., graduation, social life, studying) while on the right, under the headline, "Alumni Forever," are words that have to do with life after gradua- tion (e.g., employee benefits, starting a family, networking). Interspersed in both sections are words related to phi-

lanthropy (e.g., giving back, scholar- ships, Carolina fund).

The back of each card features messages specific to that target group. The postcards are sent to:

- **The junior class.** Farwick says in this series, 4,000 postcards were distributed. The postcard's message: next year's senior gift campaign.

- **The senior class.** This part of the postcard series educated 4,200 seniors about their Senior Class Legacy campaign. This is the only postcard that asks students to give.

- **All students (graduate and undergraduate).** This past year, the postcard was sent to 12,800 students, educating them about the role philan- thropy plays at the university.

Source: Steve Farwick, Assistant Director of Annual Giving, University of South Carolina, Columbia, SC. Phone (803) 777- 2592. E-mail: sfarwick@gwm.sc.edu

This is one design of a student philanthropy education postcard that officials at the University of South Carolina (Columbia, SC) use to encourage philanthropy among students.

Direct Mail Appeals: Donors vs. Non-donors

Q. "How should a direct mail piece aimed solely at nondonors differ from a piece that is directed toward past contributors?"

"While working with Catholic Big Brothers in Los Angeles, I once did an appeal to nondonors that used quotes from mothers whose sons had Big Brothers.

"They told, in quite poignant terms, what having a Big Brother meant to their sons."

The heartfelt appeal worked. It resulted in an 11 percent response rate, with an average gift of $86.

When appealing to nondonors, build a strong case of support, says Montgomery. Focus on the people whose lives you impact rather than your work.

"It's not your job to decide whether people will give. By not asking them, you've robbed them of the opportunity to give," he says. "Your job is to give everyone an opportunity to give."

— Gary Montgomery, Major Gifts Officer, College of Education, California State University (Sacramento, CA)

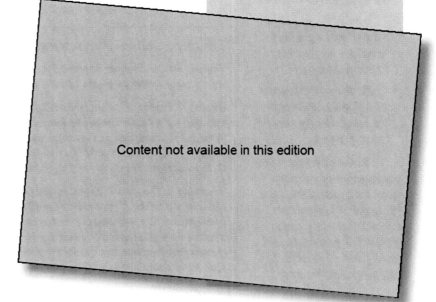

Content not available in this edition

Profitable Direct Mail Appeals: Planning, Implementing and Maximizing Results, Second Edition.
Edited by Scott C. Stevenson.
© 2009 Stevenson, Inc. Published 2009 by Stevenson, Inc.

WRITING FOR RESULTS

There are varying opinions with regard to the length of an appeal letter, what messages should be conveyed and how they are conveyed. There are, however, certain composition principles that contribute to the response rate of direct mail appeals. This chapter will some of those varying opinions as well as the guiding principles of writing for results.

Write a Simple, Concise Call to Action; Repeat

An effective fundraising appeal includes a simple and specific call to action that answers the reader's question: "Now that I care, how can I help?"

"A call to action is how the recipient can make a difference and create an impact," says Theresa Nelson, founder and principal, Theresa Nelson and Associates (Oakland, CA). "It's the place and time when you ask the recipient of the message to do something — make a donation, sign a petition, call an elected official or volunteer after a disaster."

One mistake development professionals make when writing a call to action? Overcomplicating it, says Nelson, which detracts from the message and dilutes its impact.

To write an effective call to action, Nelson says:

- Be clear and concise about what this one person can do now to make a difference.

- Use active verbs that create momentum in your message.

- Quantify the impact of the action, equating the reader's act to some specific change.

- Ask yourself, "How can I...?" Make sure your message clearly answers that question.

Additionally, repeat the message throughout your direct mail pieces, she says. "It should be in the letter at least twice, early within the first few paragraphs and usually in the postscript. It may also be on the outer envelope to preview the letter. In an e-mail, the upper-right hand portion of the body of the e-mail is considered the best position for a call-to-action box, with the message repeated in the text and often in a graphic caption."

Why so much repetition? "You need to circle back to the reason you are communicating," says Nelson. "You give the reader a reason for continuing to read, because just reading about a problem without illuminating the solution can be depressing. You need to provide for readers the answer to the question, 'Now that I care, how can I ...' at least once in the letter or e-mail text, as well as graphically. Because some people read every word of a message and others may scan only the graphics or captions, repeat the call to action in various ways to maximize the opportunity to connect with readers."

Source: Theresa Nelson, Founder and Principal, Theresa Nelson and Associates, Oakland, CA. Phone (510) 420-0539. E-mail: theresa@theresanelson.com

Inject Compelling Language Into Appeals

It's wise to write your entire year's direct mail appeals at the start of your new year to ensure key messages are incorporated into each and to demonstrate to yourself the purpose of each letter in the overall appeal process.

As you create separate appeals intended for targeted groups, incorporate persuasive language into each that legitimizes reasons for contributing, such as:

- To create a living and learning environment for tomorrow's leaders.
- To protect our natural resources for those who follow.
- To afford everyone the opportunity to experience the arts.
- To fulfill the most basic of human needs that so many of us take for granted.
- To help us achieve common acceptance of one another in a world of growing diversity.
- To show those in desperate need that we care.

Your choice of words will help legitimize why others should and will want to invest.

Effective Call-to-action Messages

Theresa Nelson, founder and principal, Theresa Nelson and Associates (Oakland, CA), shares two on-the-mark calls to action and explains why they work:

Example 1: After a recent address by President Obama on the economy, the website http://my.barackobama.com/page/content/budgetaction and coordinated e-mails said, "Watch President Obama's message and get involved in the effort to make this plan a reality by calling your elected representatives and by joining a canvass this weekend.'
Call to action: Watch the message and join a canvass this weekend.

Example 2: Doctors Without Borders seeks aid workers with the message, "Put your ideals into practice. All prospective medical and nonmedical aid workers: Join us for a presentation, film, and question-and-answer session to learn more about how you can become part of Doctors Without Borders' field work. A recruiter will be on hand to discuss requirements and the application process.' "
Call to action: Put your ideals into practice; join Doctors Without Borders in the field.

WRITING FOR RESULTS

Encourage Donors to Move Up to Next Giving Club Level

In fiscal year 2005, the University of North Carolina sent a letter to 346 former donors who had given to its annual fund the previous year at a level close to its $2,000-or-more Chancellors' Club level to encourage upgrading their current year's gift to that highest level.

Five of those donors gave enough to become Chancellors' Club members in fiscal year 2005; seven more became members in fiscal year 2006, says Rebecca Bramlett, interim assistant director of annual giving. "Overall, the piece had an 8.6 percent response rate," she says. "Thirty donors gave a total of $11,750."

These donors were first contacted through the student phonathon for a more personal solicitation, says Bramlett, and the mail piece went to those who were not contacted by phone.

The purpose of the mailing was to increase membership in the Chancellors' Club, Carolina's most generous and loyal supporters, she says. "Chancellors' Club members are recognized in an annual roster, receive regular updates about the university and are invited to special campus events. Chancellors' Club gifts may be designated to the Chancellor's University Fund (unrestricted) or to any school, academic program or department within the university."

Source: Rebecca Bramlett, Interim Assistant Director, Annual Giving, Carolina Annual Fund, University of North Carolina, Chapel Hill, NC. Phone (919) 843-3317. E-mail: Rebecca_Bramlett@unc.edu

Content not available in this edition

WRITING FOR RESULTS

Writing Effective Appeal Letters

What makes an effective appeal letter? Should it be brief or lengthy? Formal or informal?

Although there are certain principles you can follow in creating a results-oriented letter, there is a great deal of flexibility in the shape such a letter can take. Yes, there are times when a longer letter is effective. A well-organized letter that proceeds logically from opening to close, and is both interesting and compelling, will seem short despite its length. A confused and tedious letter will, on the other hand, seem long even if it's only a half page.

Here are several tips to help you improve the effectiveness of your written solicitation:

1. Have a strong sense of what your letter will say and how will look before you begin to craft your message.

2. Although your letter is a mass request for support directed to many, it ought to be perceived as a personal, informal message from one person to another. To help achieve this, focus your message on one individual, either someone you know or an imaginary composite with most of the traits of the group. Then write as if you are talking to that person.

3. Remember to be specific about what kind of response you expect, e.g., "We'd like to hear from you by Dec. 15 as we wrap up this year-end effort."

4. Your letter should ask only for one thing, but it should also provide all the information your reader needs in order to comply with your request.

5. If you're unable to personalize your salutation because of a bulk appeal, rather than "Dear Friends," consider instead an attention-getting headline, or a question that calls for a "yes" answer. (The headline/question should summon up good feelings.)

6. In the body of your letter, use simple words that speed communication. Use words that are active, concrete and colorful. Use simple, direct sentences. They move the message along.

7. Don't forget underlining or capitalization of key words or phrases (don't overdo it), handwritten inserts or marginal notes, and subheads within the body of long letters. These devices can help move the reader in your intended direction by emphasizing key words or phrases.

8. The closing and signature and title can lend authority to your message if the name is familiar or the title is prestigious.

9. The postscript can be the most effective part of the letter. You can repeat the main theme, reinforce your response deadline, or suggest a further step — like urging donors to increase their giving to certain levels.

Remember, although direct mail is probably not the best source of funds for most nonprofits, most major gifts donors started out with annual gifts in response to a letter appeal. Consider the value of your letter as a cultivation device as well as a solicitation tool.

When Writing Marketing Copy

■ Before setting out to write copy for a brochure or other marketing piece, be convinced of its primary objective. The reader's perceived message should lead to what action?

■ Keep the most important message brief. Use other portions of the piece to justify or elaborate on the key message.

Writing Tips to Make Your Job Easier

Although writing effective appeal letters is not the simplest task, here are some tips that should help make the job easier:

- **Think about your audience.** What would you tell your recipient if you had to deliver your message orally?

- **Organize your thoughts** before writing. What are the key messages you want to deliver? What do you want your message to accomplish?

- **Use conversational language.** Write the way you talk. Be direct. Check the letter's tone by reading your draft aloud.

- **Don't worry about getting it right the first time.** Write now, edit later.

Let Your Postscript Say it All

As you probably know, a direct mail appeal's postscript is one of the most important parts of your message — since it may be the only portion that gets read.

That being the case, it's important that the postscript stresses the primary objective of your appeal along with any benefits the donor will receive as a result of meeting that objective.

To select the best possible postscript, try this exercise:

1. Write down what you want the reader to do as a result of reading your letter.

2. List benefits the reader will receive in return for meeting your request.

3. Create five postscripts that incorporate this information.

4. Prioritize the postscripts and then, after getting some feedback from others, make your choice.

WRITING FOR RESULTS

Produce Appeals That Get Results

With more and more communications being sent via electronic means, personalized letters can be a nonprofit's best strategy for being noticed.

But others who seek your prospect's attention are doing the same thing, so taking a few steps to make your letter more compelling will help ensure it will be one of the first to be read.

- **Keep letters brief,** neatly spaced, error free and grammatically correct.

- **Verify spelling** of all names and proper titles of each individual.

- **Avoid use of words you wouldn't use in conversation.** You don't want to look as if you studied your thesaurus just to impress them — and you don't want your reader to have to get out the dictionary to get your message.

- **Use emotional adjectives sparingly.** Almost every appeal letter leans heavily on urgent needs and critical situations. Convey the importance of your message with less-used but still-familiar, effective words.

- **Watch punctuation.** Too many italicized, boldfaced or underlined passages clutter your page and detract from the message. Use exclamation marks only in proper context, not as an attention-getting gimmick.

- **Remember it takes more effort to write a short letter than a long one.** Ask an objective staff member to help with the editing process.

- **Don't send your first draft.** Read your letter two or three times, or until all superfluous wording is eliminated.

- **Sign your name in real ink.** Time taken to sign in a contrasting ink color shows you take a personal interest.

- **Be descriptive and direct.** Writing "our volunteers spent more than 100 hours each weekend collecting canned goods" tells your story much better than cliches such as: "We are striving to set new standards of excellence in the services we offer to those in need...."

Useful Elements for Appeal Letters

Is it time to produce another appeal letter? Unsure as to what messages to convey or what techniques you can use? Draw from among these options as you construct a message that will maximize gift returns:

- **Speak from the heart.** Sometimes, a sincere message that gets to the point is more convincing than any other approach. Write your letter as though you were having a conversation with someone.

- **Cite a fact that merits support and then build on it.** If you were surprised to learn of some fact or statistic related to your organization's work — "Our county has the highest number of teen pregnancies in the entire state," for instance — chances are it will impact the public in a similar way. Use that to build your case.

- **Focus on specific fundable projects.** Identify one or more tangible projects donors know can't happen without their gifts — computer purchases, renovation of a widely used room or creation of a program to benefit those you serve.

- **Emphasize donor benefits.** Point out how the realization of this effort will, in turn, improve your community's quality of life. Highlight direct donor benefits for gifts at various levels. Mention how gift support now will prevent future problems.

Whether you select one or a combination of these methods, it helps to review the options before haphazardly diving into an appeal message that may not be read or fully considered.

Gather Testimonials For Direct Mail Appeals

The most compelling appeals carry a message from or about those you serve. That's why it makes good sense to garner as many accounts as possible before you begin to draft your fundraising letter. To obtain the most effective endorsements, employ these approaches:

✓ Experience what your current clients are experiencing. Spend time in your customers' environments (classrooms, support groups, residential settings), to grasp what they experience. Then listen to what they're saying.

✓ Meet one on one with those you serve. Get to know your customers. Discover how their lives are impacted by your organization.

✓ Survey past customers. Whether through a formal survey, focus groups or face-to-face visits, approach past customers (graduates, former patients) to ask how your organization positively affected their lives.

Begin a file of documented testimonials you can turn to when it's time to produce a compelling appeal. Each time you come across a valuable anecdote, obtain that individual's written consent to use the testimonial and then add it to your file for future use.

Direct Mail Tip

■ When feasible, include a handwritten postscript in addition to one that is typed. Keep in mind, they will be the first two (and possibly the only two) messages to be read.

WRITING FOR RESULTS

Combine Stewardship Message With Your Appeal

Here's one approach to consider for a direct mail appeal aimed at past contributors: Before making the ask, point out the impact of the donor's last gift.

All too often, an appeal letter focuses on what's needed now with no link to past support. That's a mistake. By personalizing an appeal and helping the donor appreciate the impact made by his/her past support, he/she will be more inclined to repeat and perhaps increase future support.

Use the example below as a guide in crafting your own personalized message that points out past support and makes the case for continued and increased gifts.

```
Dear [Name]:

Last year you were one of some 1,400 friends who
collectively contributed $90,000 to our "Care for Kids"
campaign. That generosity allowed us to house and care
for 80 children who otherwise could not have afforded
our services. Your contribution has helped change their
lives for the better, and we want you to know that!

    It was in November 2008 that you contributed $80 to
this important program. Because the cost of maintaining
this program has increased — along with the number
of children who are in need of our services — we are
asking that you consider a gift of $120 this year....
```

Consider an Attention-grabbing, Stand-alone Statement

Your appeal letter should accomplish three things: 1) grab the attention of the recipient, 2) provide a compelling message and 3) move the recipient to action.

Part of the attention-grabbing element can include an opening statement or question that attracts the reader's focus and makes him/her want to learn more.

These stand-alone messages could include facts that justify your reason for asking for support: "One in eight women in our county has been abused in the past year." Or, the aim of your message may be to evoke emotion: "8-year-old Abby won't get the nutrition her body needs unless people like you care enough to step forward."

Whatever approach you take, use the stand-alone statement to grab readers' attention and begin making your case for a gift.

Hopkins Foodbank, Inc.

September 2008

Mr. & Mrs. Alden Lane
8 Richards Drive
Hopkins, AL

Dear Mr. and Mrs. Lane:

"Can you imagine what it would be like not knowing if you would be able to put food on the table for your children?"

That's the fear that a surprising number of families in our area face each day....

WRITING FOR RESULTS

Personal Stories Provide Powerful Ammunition

Annual Appeal:	Friendship Drive
Number Mailed:	10,500
Responses:	389
Average Gift:	$59

Goal:	$25,000
Raised To Date:	$22,881
Largest Gift:	$2,000

Officials with Hospice of the Panhandle, Inc. (Martinsburg, WV) have found storytelling to be a powerful way to connect with donors. Each of the organization's annual appeal letters tells a story or a combination of stories that truly illustrate how the funds are being used, says Kathie Campbell, marketing/development director.

The stories come from the patients and their families, but, Campbell says, they are careful not to use the stories of current patients and families. Instead, they interview families years after a client dies. "We seem to have the greatest response when people from our service area are profiled, but I am very reluctant to ask families directly for this type of help," says Campbell. "It's a very thin line you walk. You never want to use patients and families for your own gain."

In the past, she says, she has mailed a letter to Hospice families at least a year after the patient has died asking if they might like to help Hospice by sharing their story. "That gives them the option of considering it and initiating a call to me," she says.

Each of the Hospice's annual appeals has a theme. In a recent appeal it was "When We Needed You, You Were There." On the back of a letter signed by the organization's executive director was a list of ways that donors' contributions personally impacted patients, along with stock photos.

The year prior, the theme was "What is the most important thing we can do for you today?" On the back of a letter written on the theme were quotes in different font sizes and styles by patients who had been asked that question. Some of the responses: "I want to go fishing. I would love a hot shower. Pray for me and my family.

Just be here." A group photo of Hospice staff members accompanied the quotes.

In 1998, the theme was "Blessed Are the Piece Makers." A letter by the executive director compared Hospice to a quilt and the donors to piecemakers: "Many hands, minds and hearts contribute to one program that envelops and gives comfort." Accompanying the letter were stories by clients' families of how Hospice helped their loved one.

Source: Kathie Campbell, Marketing/Development Director, Hospice of the Panhandle, Inc., Martinsburg, WV. Phone (304) 264-0406. E-mail: kcampbell@hospiceotp.org

Advice on Writing Your Appeal

Kathie Campbell, marketing/development director, Hospice of the Panhandle, Inc. (Martinsburg, WV), shares some tips for writing effective direct mail pieces:

1. **Know your audience.** "Know who is going to read the letter and write it for them. What are they looking to hear and see?"

2. **Don't take a hard-sell approach.** "Let people get to know you and what you are about first. Let them come to you with a gift."

3. **Think low key.** "Concentrate on increasing your organization's visibility, tugging on people's heart strings and getting to know what connects people to your organization."

4. **Show your wares.** "When people see what you're about and what you're doing, you'll have a better chance of receiving a gift."

Some of the personal stories that accompanied Hospice of the Panhandle's appeal.

Content not available in this edition

WRITING FOR RESULTS

Seeking First-time Gifts? Consider Monthly Appeal

Looking to expand your annual contributor list? Consider a personalized appeal sent to different groups of non-donors each month of the year. Directing a highly personalized letter to a different group of non-donors each month, you can:

✓ Target specific groups of individuals and/or businesses each month (e.g., particular ZIP codes, professions, interest groups).

✓ Make your letter more timely. If you're preparing a November letter, for example, your message might make reference to Thanksgiving.

✓ Test different appeal letters and funding projects to determine which produce the best responses.

✓ Generate new gift revenue on an ongoing basis. Instead of two different appeals going out twice each year, this approach, if successful, should provide your organization with ongoing gift revenue from new sources.

Let Donors Write Your Appeals

Ever get writer's block when it's time to draft that next appeal?

Try looking to your volunteers and donors for sustenance. Meet with a handful of individuals who are sold on your organization and what it does. Ask them why they believe in your programs and services. List specific reasons for their belief in your nonprofit.

Chances are their perceptions will provide the raw material you've been looking for and will inspire you in writing the appeal. Their ability to look from the outside in can provide the ways in which your nonprofit is meeting the needs of the community or region. Listen carefully to what they say. Their natural responses to your questions may provide key words or phrases that bring a new vitality to your solicitation message.

In addition to gathering good marketing material, you've also just cultivated a stronger relationship with those whose advice you sought, making them even better volunteers and/or donors.

Direct Mail Tip

Whether you're crafting a two-page direct mail appeal or writing copy for an annual fund brochure, get to the point.

Tell readers what it is you want of them in your opening statement. Then, if you're lucky enough to have them read on, you can provide supporting material.

Unfortunately, far too many letters and brochures go on and on and never get to the point.

Effective Writing Tip

■ After finishing a piece of writing, leave it alone for a while. If possible, don't look at it for at least 24 hours. Then go back and reread it.

By letting it sit for a while, it will be as if you're looking at it for the first time. This procedure will help you spot any errors or changes needed to make your initial draft even better.

Phrases That Convey Urgency

If your letter needs to convey urgency, here are some phrases to consider —

• Time is running out.
• Please make your contribution today.
• They're depending on you!
• Their lives can't wait any longer.
• It's in your hands. Please do it now.
• It's now or never. You be the judge.
• This can't go on any longer.
• They cry out for your help.
• If you can't help, who can?
• Help reverse this destructive trend.
• Can you live with their demise?

Appeal Writing Tips

• While an appeal letter may convey a sense of urgency, don't overdo it to the point of sounding desperate. Although people like to know their gifts are making a noticeable difference, they also want to believe the cause they are supporting will exist a year or a decade from now.

• If you're approaching someone with celebrity status to sign an appeal letter (e.g., board member, community leader, corporate CEO), why not take it a step further? Get his/her commitment to personally thank the 25 largest contributors who respond to the letter.

Profitable Direct Mail Appeals: Planning, Implementing and Maximizing Results, Second Edition.
Edited by Scott C. Stevenson.
© 2009 Stevenson, Inc. Published 2009 by Stevenson, Inc.

KEY PACKAGE COMPONENTS

While the sum of the parts, the contents of each direct mail appeal will impact overall gift results. Each piece within that package — letter, brochure, pledge form, outer envelope, return envelope — will contribute to the appeal's overall success or failure. Each component within the package should have a relationship to the remaining pieces.

Use Response Cards With Direct Mail, Face-to-face Calls

Every face-to-face or direct mail contact you have with people should allow you to invite their involvement with your organization in some capacity. Whether meeting with a first-time or long-time donor, the individual's growing involvement with your institution is the single most important factor in generating new or increased gifts, needed volunteer assistance, or both.

So what systems do you have in place that help to show you when someone may be interested? How do you know when someone might want to establish a scholarship? How do you know someone wants to get involved in planning a special event? When someone is willing to assist in your capital campaign?

The use of response cards or bounce backs should be incorporated whenever and wherever possible.

Whenever a new brochure is developed, include an accompanying response card. Whenever correspondence is sent, include a response card. Whenever you meet with anyone, select a response card that best fits the circumstances and share it with the prospect.

The response card gives others a tangible reason to get back to you. And when they do, you don't have to guess or read minds. You have evidence that they have expressed interest in learning more about your organization and perhaps, how they can assist your efforts.

As you can see from the examples here, there is no limit on the number of ways in which you can use this simple tool. Assess the many ways in which bounce backs may be useful in your work.

Examples of bouncebacks that can accompany various types of brochures and mailings.

Pleased to meet you..... Let's get to know each other

Name _____
Address _____
City _____ State ____ ZIP _____
Day Phone _____
Evening Phone _____
Occupation _____ Title _____

I'm interested in learning more about the following

- ☐ The college's history and mission
- ☐ Distinguishing achievements of the college
- ☐ Course offerings/majors
- ☐ Career advising
- ☐ Financial aid/scholarship assistance
- ☐ Upcoming calendar of events
- ☐ Speakers bureau topics
- ☐ Volunteer opportunities
- ☐ Exploring planned gift opportunities
- ☐ Annual fund opportunities
- ☐ Endowed gift opportunities
- ☐ How to establish a scholarship
- ☐ The college's future plans
- ☐ Alumni activities and involvement
- ☐ Distinguished graduates of the institution
- ☐ Status of the endowment
- ☐ Other _____

Learn More About How to Establish a Scholarship

Name _____
Address _____
City _____ State ____ ZIP _____
Day Phone _____
Evening Phone _____
Occupation _____ Title _____

I would like to learn more about establishing or adding to a named scholarship. Please provide me with additional information on the following topic(s):

- ☐ How scholarships help students
- ☐ How scholarships help the college
- ☐ How scholarships help our society
- ☐ How to establish a named scholarship
- ☐ Using memorial gifts to establish a _____ scholarship
- ☐ Annual scholarships and how they work
- ☐ Endowed scholarships and how they work
- ☐ Placing restrictions on scholarships
- ☐ Establishing or adding to a scholarship through my estate
- ☐ Selection of scholarship recipients
- ☐ Meeting the recipients of my scholarship
- ☐ Potential tax benefits of establishing a scholarship

Use Phrases as Envelope Teasers

Do you ever include a teaser on the outer envelope of your direct mail appeal? If having a teaser will get more mail opened, it's worth testing. Here are some examples:

- Special offer for new donors.
- Limited time offer.
- Our community needs help.
- Lives are at stake.
- Important information enclosed.
- Are you the one who will make the difference?
- There are hungry people in our community.
- Your personal membership card.
- It's not too late to join this year's effort.
- Premium enclosed.
- Confidential.
- Our county ranks highest in teen pregnancies.
- With your help we can do it.
- We're really counting on you.
- You're the one.
- Stop violence now.
- If you don't, who will?
- It's your choice.
- It's that time of year.
- Urgent news inside.
- Insider's report.
- Please show you care.
- Give for those who will follow.
- Personal.

Envelope Acronyms —

In the direct mail appeal world there are two envelope types: The business reply envelope (BRE) and the courtesy reply envelope (CRE).

The difference: the BRE has your organization's address and is postage-paid while, although the CRE is also a pre-addressed envelope, the donor is asked to supply the stamp.

KEY PACKAGE COMPONENTS

Don't Underestimate Value of A Wish List

Consider making a wish list a part of your next direct mail package. This component will offer a snapshot of your organization's most pressing needs, while reducing the number of direct mail appeals for individual projects and reducing costs.

The Jewish Historical Society of Greater Washington (Washington, DC) had great success by incorporating a wish list into its bi-annual newsletter.

This list (reproduced in part, right) includes a brief description of each item and its cost. Values range from $136 for a volunteer training manual to $25,000 for a living history program that recreates an historic 19th century wedding.

Executive Director Laura Apelbaum says they base the ask amount on actual cost; administrative overhead is built in for program-related items. Items are categorized by need (e.g., archives and research, education and programming, office needs).

Apelbaum says they usually receive two to three gifts each time the wish list is published in the newsletter.

"Members occasionally complain that we send out too many requests for funds for individual projects," she says. "This technique allows us to reach all of our members in a less 'threatening' way — they can look at the list and decide to give without being solicited."

Wish lists in a recent newsletter yielded $300 to take photos of a historic building; $1,400 for wooden folding chairs and $2,500 for oral histories. The spring list yielded a $1,800 gift to mount an online exhibit and $3,000 to fund the next edition of the newsletter.

The list encourages members to give special gifts that are much higher than their membership levels and identifies new prospective major donors, she says. "This year, a member came forward to fund the online exhibit for $1,800 when she had previously been a member at a standard level."

To populate the wish list, Apelbaum asks staff for suggestions, then prioritizes requested items from most to least urgent.

"We look for items with a range of cost," she says. "We usually look for items that are $500 or more. It seems to maximize the return and avoids two donors wanting to fund the same item."

Wish list donors are sent a thank you and acknowledged in the next newsletter.

Source: Laura Apelbaum, Executive Director, Jewish Historical Society, Washington, DC. Phone (202) 789-0900. E-mail: laura@jhsgw.org

Content not available in this edition

Check, Then Choose Best Way to Communicate

Some people prefer being contacted via e-mail. Others may favor postal mail. Still others might choose a phone call to their business or home.

If you haven't yet done so, ask persons on your mailing list — at least major contributors — which communications method(s) they prefer. You'll not only be telling them you put their interests first, but by honoring their choice, you'll increase the odds of getting your messages noticed.

Ask for communications preferences periodically and in varied ways: bounce-backs included with other mailings, on your website, during one-on-one visits, etc. At right is a simple sample of text you could include on a return post card you could include in your direct mail appeal:

Content not available in this edition

KEY PACKAGE COMPONENTS

Include 'In Memory' and 'In Honor of' Opportunities

Although some pledge cards and envelopes get far too cluttered, you may wish to consider the appropriateness of listing "in memory of" and "in honor of" pledges on your form. In fact, you may want to include multiple pledge opportunities that address these categories. This example illustrates tribute gift opportunities that could be included on your pledge form:

This gift/tribute is:

In memory of _____

_____

In honor of _____

On the occasion of _____

In celebration of _____

Other (specify) _____

Please send notice of my gift/tribute to:

Name _____

Address _____

City _____

State _____ Zip _____

ST. JOHN'S
MEDICAL CENTER

Six Alternatives To 'Affix Postage Here'

Do you ask your donors to use their own stamps to mail a business reply envelope or postcard? If so, here are alternatives to putting "Affix Postage Here" in the stamp area help explain why you do so:

1. "Your stamp helps us here, too."

2. "Your gift begins with a stamp"

3. "Your stamp adds to your support!"

4. "Your gift begins here."

5. "Your stamp on the return envelope is an additional 42-cent gift to us."

6. "Your donation starts here."

New Donor Packet Encourages Repeat Giving

Last year, Albion College officials began sending new donor packets to their new annual donors. The packets include a wall calendar, a list of campus phone numbers, a change of address postcard, a BRE, a luggage tag promotional flyer, two or three trinkets (e.g., a sticker, a pen, a "Thanks" magnet, etc.) and a letter from the director of annual giving.

"The director's letter highlights the benefits of being a donor (e.g., an invitation to the opening convocation lecture series, access to the online alumni directory, etc.)," says Emily Ernsberger, assistant director of alumni/parent relations and annual giving. "I make sure that we hand address the envelopes and that they are received within three weeks of processing the gift."

So far, says Ernsberger, the packets have been well received. Twenty-nine percent of new donors who received the packets in the 2004/2005 fiscal year made a second gift in fiscal year 2005/2006, she says.

Depending on what is including in the packet, says Ernsberger, each cost about $2 to mail.

Source: Emily Ernsberger, Assistant Director of Alumni/Parent Relations and Annual Giving, Albion College, Albion, MI. Phone (517) 629-0829. E-mail: eernsberger@albion.edu

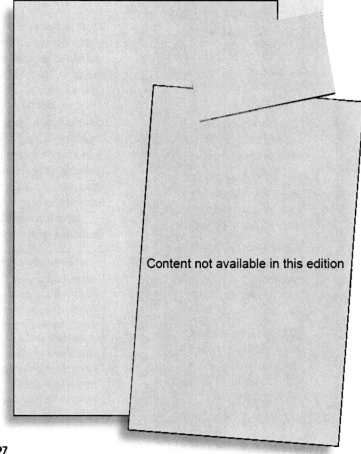

Content not available in this edition

KEY PACKAGE COMPONENTS

Mention Online Giving on All Pledge Forms

Do all of your pledge forms invite donors to make online contributions? It's wise to include that option since it might be perceived by some as being easier than writing a check and mailing it. Plus, online gifts save you postage.

Also, if your online giving program makes it possible, consider instructing donors to fill in a particular coupon code that allows them to receive a special premium as a thank you for their generosity. By doing this, you can track the gift to a particular direct mail effort to measure its response rate.

YES, I/we wish to support the YMCA with a gift of $ _____

☐ Enclosed is my check.

Please charge $ _____ to my credit card.
☐ VISA ☐ MasterCard ☐ American Express ☐ Discover
Exp. Date _____
Acct # _____
Name _____
Address _____ State _____ Zip _____
City _____
Home Ph _____ Business Ph _____
E-mail _____

Forget the envelope! Give online at www.ymcaanywhereusa.org

Outer Envelope Plays A Role in Response

✓ Your envelope should match the tone of the appeal and should entice readers to open it.

✓ To ensure the envelopes get opened, address the envelopes by hand.

✓ Consider using a teaser on your envelope, but remember, a poor teaser is worse than no teaser.

✓ If you're mailing bulk rate, consider using bulk-rate stamps as opposed to a meter tape or mailing indicia.

✓ If you're mailing first class, consider using a commemorative stamp that has meaning for your organization.

Include Mission Statement On Pledge Forms

Most advancement professionals will agree: For would-be donors to buy into and invest in your organization, they first must have a clear understanding of your mission.

One way to inform potential contributors of your mission and add legitimacy to your request for support is to include it on all pledge forms (assuming the statement is concise; otherwise, consider an abbreviated version for this purpose).

Here is a sample pledge form that includes a mission statement:

Avoid Critical Offer Mistakes

While many components will contribute to your appeal letter's success (or failure), none is as important as the offer. What are you offering the would-be contributor that will cause him/her to make a gift? Be sure your offer avoids these mistakes:

- **An offer that is not specific.** Avoid vagueness that conveys all gifts end up in a "big black hole." Offer specific funding projects with which donors can identify.

- **An offer with no value.** Are you asking to help pay the bills? Or are you providing the chance to make a noticeable difference in the lives of those you serve? Point out how gifts will benefit those making the donations.

- **An offer that is not unique.** Any educational facility can ask for scholarships. Why not ask for science scholarships for females? Any hospital can ask for assistance treating patients. Why not ask for help treating children with cancer?

Your Generosity Is Appreciated — LINWOOD HOSPICE

Our Mission: To make hospice care available to all patients and families in the Linwood area without regard to race, creed, gender, or ability to pay. In providing care to persons with a limited life expectancy, hospice neither attempts to prolong life nor to hasten death.

Please sign and complete the following information
Name(s) _____
Address _____
City _____ State _____ Zip _____
☐ I wish to remain anonymous
Form of Payment
☐ Enclosed is my check for $_____ (Make checks payable to *Linwood Hospice*.)
☐ Credit card. Please charge my credit card in the amount of $_____
☐ Discover ☐ Visa ☐ Mastercard ☐ American Express
Card No. _____ Expiration _____
Signature _____

TRY AND TEST NEW IDEAS

Because of each charity's uniqueness and special circumstances, it's important to keep trying and testing new ideas with each direct mail appeal. Try new messages, new ways of packaging your appeal, new funding projects. Equally important, monitor and evaluate the results of each idea and each test.

25 Percent Increase in Programming Justifies Request for Equal Increase in Giving

Have you ever used an increase in services you provide to justify asking for an equal increase in financial support?

In fall 2001, California Symphony officials expanded their concert series by 25 percent and then ran a direct mail campaign asking donors to increase their giving by 25 percent. The campaign, called "25% More Music For the Soul," was sent to 2,146 donors of less than $1,000, subscribers, single ticket buyers and lapsed donors from past years. The result? The campaign raised $16,928 from 132 donors.

"The campaign raised 12.44 percent more money than the previous year," says Juli Kramer, director of development. "The average gift was $128.24, an increase of 7.56 percent over the previous year's average gift."

In addition to the approach she used for the appeal, Kramer attributes the campaign's success to the following:

- Personalization of the letters using first names and the amount of their previous gift (when appropriate).
- Printing the signature of the music director in blue ink.
- Using invitation-sized solicitation pieces with an RSVP note printed on the front of the outer envelope.

Source: Juli Kramer, Director of Development, California Symphony, Pleasant Hill, CA. Phone (925) 280-2490. E-mail: jkramer@californiasymphony.org

Try Testing 'Back-to-back' Appeals

Think of all the junk mail you receive at home. Much of it hardly gets a glance before it's off to the trash. And sometimes mail you may have read in other circumstances — more time on your hands, less stressed, etc. — gets lumped in with the junk mail.

That's the same way many of those to whom you send an appeal might react. Under some circumstances your letter will get pitched without even having been opened, while in others, the recipient might read it and positively respond with a gift. That's why you should periodically test back-to-back mailings to the same group.

Send an appeal to a smaller segment of your mailing list. Then, say 30 or 45 days later, send another appeal to those in the same group who didn't respond to the first mailing. Begin the second letter with a messages such as: "Just in case you missed our first invitation to support an important and deserving project...."

Measure the response of both mailings. Evaluate items such as percentage that responded with a gift to each mailing; average gift size; number of responses; amount generated from each mailing; cost/revenue ratio; etc. Then weigh those stats against any negative responses you received from those who received two mailings in a row.

By testing back-to-back appeals with smaller groups, you can determine whether to use that method for a larger scale campaign.

Test New Mailing Options

Q: "We would like to stop using BREs (postage-paid business reply envelopes), but are concerned that we will lose donors as a result. What has been your experience after eliminating BREs?"

"We stopped using BREs several years ago. We made no announcements or references to the change. I received no complaints and no discernible drop-off in gifts. If someone is truly philanthropic, a $39-cent stamp isn't going to preclude him or her from sending you a $25 or $50 check. Those opposed to postage may give online anyway.

"Even if you have a slight drop-off from a gift or two, you may be ahead by not spending the money on postage for all the gifts you receive. You can use that postage savings somewhere else to generate even more gifts."

— James Spencer, Coordinator of Major Gifts and Planned Giving, Rowan University (Glassboro, NJ)

Follow-up Appeal Messages

Use follow-up messages on both your outer envelope and your letter's opening statement....

✓ We missed hearing back from you.

✓ Your absence was noticed.

✓ It won't be the same without your participation.

✓ Just in case you overlooked our first invitation....

TRY AND TEST NEW IDEAS

Test Direct Mail Pieces Head to Head

Before pursuing a direct mail campaign, test its various elements to determine what package and message will resonate best with the widest audience possible.

Tim Crum, director of marketing and development, PetSmart Charities (Phoenix, AZ), says it's imperative to know what you are trying to accomplish for each individual campaign (e.g., maximize net revenue, maximize responses, increase average gift, reactivate lapsed donors, etc.).

"Determining which package, message and the organization's goal all play a key role in producing the best possible return on investment," Crum says.

To achieve the most effective direct mail piece, he says, test five elements:

1. **Package.** What does the piece look like? On the outside (color, size, photos, teaser copy)? And on the inside (letter, reply piece, insert)?

2. **Story.** What are you trying to say? How do you want the recipient to feel?

3. **Ask.** What action do you want the recipient to take?

4. **Timing.** How often are you mailing? When was the last campaign mailing? When is the next one?

5. **List.** To whom are you sending this?

Measure each element in a head-to-head test to allow an analyst to isolate what works and what does not, Crum says. Testing several elements in one campaign can bring convoluted results and may not accurately reveal what element was successful.

Test these elements, Crum says:

- **Package.** Test teaser versus non-teaser copy; photo versus none; insert versus none.

- **Story.** Test 4-page letter versus 2-page; emotion-based story-telling versus fact-based list of programs, services.

- **Ask.** Test gift array versus non-gift array; various size options versus none.

- **Timing.** Track what stories are sent and when and their results.

- **List.** Test different rented lists to see which audience works best.

Source: Tim Crum, Director of Marketing and Development, PetSmart Charities, Phoenix, AZ. Phone (623) 587-2658. E-mail: TCrum@PetSmartCharities.org

---

Back-end Premium Boosts Average Gift Size

Encouraging givers to give a bit more is often worth the effort.

At PetSmart Charities (Phoenix, AZ), Tim Crum, director of marketing and development, teamed up with Lisa Goin, manager of annual giving, to create a direct mail campaign that offered donors of $50 to $75 a back-end premium for giving $100 or more.

The campaign was designed to test how many donors would upgrade to the $100 gift level with the offer of a premium gift.

"PetSmart Charities, up to this point, had difficulty in getting this segment of our donors to increase its donations," he says. "This particular method proved to be a very effective way for our organization to upgrade donors."

The direct mail campaign resulted in an average gift size from the back-end premium test of $89.87 in May of 2006 compared to the average gift of $25.92 for all of the organization's donor mailings that year — an increase of nearly 350 percent.

Two Cardinal Rules For Successful Appeals

After working as both an annual fund director and in his current position as Director of Athletics Development, David T. Trueb of The University of Alabama (Huntsville, AL) has developed a couple of rules for mail solicitations.

Rule 1: Divide and conquer. "Don't let one letter suffice for your entire mailing list," says Trueb. "It's better to segment your list and create different letters for each. The best step we ever took with the annual fund was sending out letters from each department with a department chair's signature as well as the dean's. We even went so far as to remove athletics alumni from department lists and substituted coaches' letters instead."

Rule 2: Show them the meat. Trueb says the appearance of the appeal letter is important when it comes to direct mail. "We've found donors more interested in seeing students' faces and hearing about students' success and less about wants and needs."

He says the school conducted a very successful spring appeal a few years ago featuring a family of alumni. "The letter was written by the father of eight alums who collectively held more than 11 degrees from UAH. We included a series of photos of the children with their degrees and names listed as part of the letterhead. These third-party testaments add much more credibility than anything we can do."

Source: David T. Trueb, Director, Athletics Development, The University of Alabama in Huntsville, Huntsville, AL. Phone (256) 824-6584. E-mail: Truebd@email.uah.edu

TRY AND TEST NEW IDEAS

Add Personalized Brochure in Your Annual Fund Mailings

The more personal you can make a mailing, the better the chance the recipient will open it, read it and lend support to your cause.

Bridget Snow, principal and creative director, Bridget Snow Design (Warwick, RI), says an alternative to a traditional personalized letter and mass-produced brochure is a personalized brochure using variable data printing — a form of on-demand printing that lets you change text, graphics and images within individual pieces in a single database or external file in the same print run.

This mailer shows how certain aspects can be personalized, from recipient to photos to specific messages.

"Tastefully crafting a tailored personalized brochure can grab an individual reader's interest, and is in some cases more effective than the standard personalized letter, which has saturated the marketplace," says Snow. Variables can include message changes according to giving level; photos/graphics and specific messages and visuals specific to academic/extracurricular activities.

Snow says two factors determine cost-effectiveness of variable data printing: total press run and number of customized elements.

These examples show how quantity and number of customizations impact cost:

Project: Four-color, self-mailer for independent school's annual fund campaign.
Total run: 5,000 pieces in lots of 3,500 and 1,500, each requiring variable imagery.
Option A: Traditionally printed four-color process on two sides; variable black plate on both sides.

Option B: Traditionally printed four-color process on one side; variable black on both sides and variable four-color on one side.

Snow says the Option B quote came in higher by 40 percent.

Project: Reunion invitation
Total run: 800 pieces, comprising 11 sets of variables in four-color, self-mailer.
Option A: Traditional four-color process and a variable black plate.
Option B: All variable four-color process.

Snow says that because quantity was a significant production factor, using totally variable printing the job (Option B) cost 21 percent less than Option A.

Source: Bridget Snow, Principal/Creative Director, Bridget Snow Design, Warwick, RI. Phone (401) 781-2224.
E-mail: bsnow@bsnowdesign.com.
Website: www.bsnowdesign.com

Survey Reveals Need To Retool Appeal

Surveys to both donors and past donors can bring about needed changes in fundraising strategies.

When participation in direct mail appeals started to drop, annual giving staff at Oberlin College (Oberlin, OH) wanted to know why, so they created a survey and sent it to alumni with active e-mail addresses (about half of the solicitable database). The results revealed some interesting information.

According to Donna Ancypa Holmes, assistant director, The Oberlin Fund, "the survey not only asked about their attitudes toward giving, but how effective our appeals were and who they preferred to hear from — the president, a member of the board of trustees or a faculty member."

What officials discovered was that the general appeal wasn't specific enough. "People wanted more information," says Holmes.

Other changes are in the works, too. "Now we're changing the format to emphasize messages that are more meaningful to our donors and more likely to motivate them to give," for example, preserving the value of an Oberlin education or reflecting the values that led them to choose Oberlin in the first place, says Holmes.

College officials also need 1,300 additional annual donors to bring their participation rate back up to speed, so they're considering fulfillment gifts — a bumper sticker or some other item — as possible incentives.

Source: Donna Ancypa Holmes, Assistant Director, The Oberlin Fund, Oberlin College, Oberlin, OH. Phone (440) 775-5536. E-mail: donna.ancypa.holmes@oberlin.edu

Profitable Direct Mail Appeals — 2nd Edition: Planning, Implementing and Maximizing Results

IMPROVE YOUR RESPONSE RATE

The rationale behind testing and trying new ideas is ultimately to improve your appeal's response rate. But know in advance exactly what it is you want to improve. Net revenue? Cost to revenue ratio? Average gift size? Increased numbers of donors? Retention of past donors? Pledge fulfillment rate? All of these are important to varying degrees.

Boost Your Appeal's Response Rate With a 'Johnson Box'

One way to get the key message of your direct mail solicitation letter heard is by using a "Johnson Box."

A Johnson Box, placed at the very top of the letter above the salutation, is a centered, rectangular box containing the key message that you want your reader to remember most. Pioneer direct mail copywriter Frank H. Johnson created the Johnson Box some 60 years ago.

Ivan Levison, Direct Response Copywriting (Greenbrae, CA), shares five tips for getting the most out of using a Johnson Box:

1. **Include the right content.** The Johnson Box could contain a quote, the special reason you're contacting them now or an important announcement.

2. **Use it in the right kind of letter.** If you're sending a non-personalized letter that's going out bulk rate in a window envelope using teaser copy, a Johnson Box will fit right in. But if you're writing a first-class letter in a closed-face envelope, the Johnson Box will

look cheap and out of place.

3. **Make it the right size.** If you're mailing an 8 1/2 X 11-inch letter (folded twice down to 3 5/8-inches), you want the Johnson Box, and at least the salutation line, to appear above the fold. Two-inches deep by 3 1/2-inches wide is reasonable, but there's no firm rule.

4. **Use an appropriate box shape.** You can make the box out of asterisks (*) or a fine-ruled line. You might even want to add color inside the box.

5. **Include a Johnson Box in your next e-mail solicitation.** Run a line above and below the text rather than enclosing it in a box. The Johnson box should fit easily into the reader's auto-preview box.

Source: Ivan Levison, Direct Response Copywriting, Greenbrae, CA.
Phone (415) 461-0672.
E-mail: ivan@levison.com

```
These children need your help.
And they need it now!
```

Develop Second-time Follow-up Procedures

As you keep testing new ways to produce the best direct-mail results for your appeals, don't overlook the "second-time follow-up" approach.

With this method, the appeal is first sent to your intended audience. Then, after sufficient time has elapsed for donors to respond, say four weeks, a second appeal is sent to all of those who did not respond to your first mailing.

To cut printing expenses, print sufficient envelopes, return envelopes

and letterhead at one time to cover needs for both mailings. The only thing that might change will be your message on the second appeal: "Mary, we realize you're busy and may have simply forgot to respond to our first appeal for support, so we're contacting you once again to invite you to invest in this important cause."

You'll find that this cost-effective repeat method will increase your overall response rate.

Personal Notes Quadruple Letter's Response Rate

Dan De Vries, director of development, The National Center for Youth Law (Oakland, CA) has found that adding personal touches to basic direct mail letters pays off.

The center began attaching personal, handwritten notes to direct mail appeal letters in 1993, and by 2001, direct mail revenue more than quadrupled. The personal touch is also effective in retaining donors. "Some donors have given every year since we started attaching personal notes," says De Vries. "People realize we're paying personal attention to them, and that strengthens their identification with our program."

Each note is written by someone within the organization who knows the donor or prospect. The center's director alone has a list of 744 prospects or donors whom he personally knows. Most of the director's notes simply read, "I hope you can help." Other times he may have something more specific or personal to say to a donor.

Source: Dan De Vries, Director of Development, The National Center For Youth Law, Oakland, CA. Phone (510) 835-8098, ext. 3008. E-mail: ddv@youthlaw.org

IMPROVE YOUR RESPONSE RATE

Create Appeals Designed to Upgrade Donors' Gifts

How much planning do you put into getting existing donors to upgrade their giving from year to year?

Mass appeals to an entire donor constituency just don't cut it anymore. It's important that you take a targeted approach in convincing donors to give more to your worthwhile cause this year than they did last year.

Experiment with these methods designed to upgrade donors' giving:

1. Produce personalized appeals that state what the donor gave last year, then ask for a specific increase.

2. Develop a separate appeal letter for each of your giving levels or clubs. If, for instance, you have a $100 to 250 level, craft an appeal that makes the case for contributing at the next higher level. In addition to pointing out donor benefits associated with that gift club or level, inform your audience that all gifts given at that level will be used for a specific — and appealing — purpose.

3. Send a second or third appeal to current donors at midyear or during your fourth quarter, pointing out what they have contributed thus far and letting them know how much more they would need to give to move into the next donor level.

Appeal Letter Uses Celebrity Signers Tied to Mission

The Korean War Veterans National Museum and Library has had much success with a direct mail letter signed by Astronaut Buzz Aldrin, a Korean War veteran. "We were hoping to break even with the mailing, but we are doing much better than that," says Larry Sassorossi, executive director.

The purpose of the mailing was to accumulate 20,000 names in the first year to develop their own in-house mailing list. "We have already accumulated almost 13,000 names," says Sassorossi. "Plus, we have made a modest profit."

Museum officials sent some 1.5 million pieces in 2004 during a multi-phase campaign that includes several different direct mail letters signed by celebrities or notable people with ties to the Korean War. They sent the first Buzz Aldrin letter to 40,000 people. Of that, 5,000 letters were then sent to eight groups as a test. They recently mailed out 400,000 pieces to 12 different groups.

All mailings received about a 2 percent response rate, says Sassorossi. Also since then, they have sent out an additional 760,000 letters to 37 different groups. The results of that mailing are still coming in. The average gift from all mailings so far has been $41.

The direct mail company that the museum hired to help with the campaign jointly suggested names for the celebrity signer. "We settled on Buzz Aldrin as our first celebrity signer because veterans love him and he is a veteran himself," he says. "We contacted him, told him what we were trying to do, and asked him to participate, and he said yes.

"When using a celebrity signer I think it's important to find a neutral person with no political or cause-related agenda. You don't want to give someone a reason not to give."

Source: Larry Sassorossi, Executive Director, Korean War Veterans National Museum and Library, Highland Park, IL. Phone (888) 295-7212. E-mail: Larrysasso@kwvm.com

Pledge Fulfillment Tips

While you are no doubt familiar with credit cards as a viable way to accept contributions, here are two tips to increase contributions:

- Add blanks for credit card payments on all pledge reminders.

- Mention the credit card option on all solicitations — direct mail appeals, phonathons and face-to-face calls.

- For multi-year pledges, encourage credit card donors to initiate pre-authorized debits that allow you to debit their cards over a specified period of time.

Why Allow Credit Card Payments?

If you still have doubts about offering credit card payments as a way for donors to contribute, consider that credit cards are not only convenient, but they:

- Encourage larger gifts since quarterly or monthly gifts are often more palatable than a single large annual gift.

- Are a preferred way to pay for many online donors.

- Usually make for larger than traditional cash gifts.

- Create another payment option, increasing the odds that you'll boost your overall number of donations.

Content not available in this edition

IMPROVE YOUR RESPONSE RATE

Reach Into the Response Rate Tool Chest

We're all looking for ways to increase the response rate for direct mail. We've pulled together a chest of direct mail tools that will help you do just that!

Planning Your Mailing....

☐ Use different letters for donors than for prospective donors. Donors should be treated like insiders and nondonors should be encouraged to join the team.

☐ Segment your mailing list and target key groups for gifts directed to specific projects.

☐ Consider a series of appeals as opposed to a one-shot request.

☐ Make your mailings timely — tie them to special events like holidays or organizational events.

☐ Consider a campaign slogan that ties each piece within your direct mail package.

Writing the Letter....

☐ Write your letter as if you're sending it to one person using a conversational style.

☐ Deliver the most important message in the first paragraph. Make it compelling and to the point.

☐ Use action words throughout your appeal that result in vivid mental images.

☐ Use statistics that are believable as well as accurate — and use them sparingly.

☐ Illustrate how gifts will make a difference. Better yet, tell them what past gifts did to make a difference. Give them specific examples.

☐ Use headlines or boldface type to bring attention to important messages.

☐ Convey urgency in your letter, and set a deadline: "We need to hear from you by May 31 so your name can be included in the annual honor roll of contributors."

☐ Carefully select the individual who will sign your letter. You may be further ahead to consider a client who has benefited from your organization or a visible and respected volunteer.

☐ Try to keep paragraphs short to ensure ease of reading. It will help them complete the letter.

☐ Include a postscript that repeats an important message. It's sometimes the only portion of the letter that gets read!

☐ Ask a respected colleague to read your completed letter to review its impact, flow and grammar.

Completing the Direct Mail Package....

☐ Develop a reply or pledge card that stands on its own. Readers will misplace or toss your letter more likely than the reply card.

☐ Consider using a teaser on your envelope, but remember, a poor teaser is worse than no teaser.

☐ If you're mailing bulk rate, consider using bulk-rate stamps as opposed to a meter tape or mailing indicia. It looks less like junk mail.

☐ If you're mailing first class, consider using a commemorative stamp that has meaning for your organization.

☐ When possible, address envelopes by hand for a more personal look.

☐ Before your package is printed, have more than one individual proof each piece by reading backwards.

Make Gift and Member Club Names Distinctive

What are the names of your various gift clubs or membership levels? How long have they been in existence?

If the names of your gift clubs or membership levels are as uninspired as many seem to be — Century Club, Gold Club, President's Club, etc. — it may be time for an overhaul. After all, these various levels are created to entice donors/members, not oppress them.

Get together with staff first and then your development or membership committee. Identify several distinctive possibilities based on various levels of support and accompanying benefits. As you brainstorm ideas, consider:

1. The name of someone who made a significant difference in the life of your organization — former employee, board member, donor. Example: The Hawthorn Society.

2. Names unique to your organization's purpose or mission. Examples:

   • An orchestra — The Quintet Club, The Symphonic Society, etc.

   • An environmental organization — The Oak Tree Guild, The Acorn Alliance, etc.

3. Names unique to your community or region.

4. Names tied to a point in history or the history of your organization.

   In addition to being distinctive, club or membership level names should make the right fit with each increasing level.

IMPROVE YOUR RESPONSE RATE

Three Ways to Increase Direct Mail Response Rates

Do you want to generate more gift revenue from your direct mail appeals? Check out what these professionals did:

Educate. "Over the past three to four years, we focused on educating existing donors, prospects, event attendees and select acquisitions on Children's Trust Fund and our work. We did this in conjunction with an integrated marketing campaign (i.e., statewide billboards, e-communications, newsletters and personal notes). We are receiving donations from people who have never given and have been on our lists for more than 10 years!"

> — *Jodi Wolin,*
> *Chief Development Officer,*
> *Massachusetts Children's Trust Fund*
> *(Boston, MA)*

Personalize. "With some clients, we use program information that is personalized to their geographic location. In other cases, we use giving history to personalize a specific thank-you for past support. There are also production techniques for larger mailings that allow us to use a donor or prospect's name throughout a mail piece for a more personal connection to the copy. Try to be more personal with donors and let them know you know who they are and that you appreciate them."

> — *Catherine M. Connolly, Independent Consultant (Sacramento, CA)*

Reflect. "Normally an annual report is something that is required but not money producing. Our annual report was a reflection of the long-term stability of the organization, but also raised the question, 'Will they be around next year?' We made our report a story of how we were making a difference and used examples and pictures. We added a letter from the CEO, a donation envelope and I signed a promise to keep the organization's focus on helping people to help themselves. We got more than $400,000 in donations from that direct mailing!"

> — *Mike Sullivan, Development Director, ECHO (North Fort Myers, FL)*

Add Spice to Your Pledge Billings

When you send monthly or quarterly billings to those with outstanding pledges, do you include anything with the statements?

Why not make pledge billings something enjoyable to receive? By including items — such as those listed below — your fulfillment rate may actually increase. Here are a handful of examples that could be included with your pledge billings:

- Calendars of upcoming events.
- Return cards that offer planned gift materials, advice.
- A copy of a recent news release.
- Free tickets or a memento with your logo imprinted on it.
- Memorial and in-tribute cards to encourage such gifts.
- A list of your organization's recent achievements.

- A fact card that concisely profiles your organization or some particular program.
- Your organization's wish list of additional gift opportunities.

Bounce Backs Increase Response Rate

It's wise to send appeals, or any communication for that matter, that invite persons to respond or, "bounce back." By involving people in your piece, you're more likely to see them include a gift with their response.

Here are methods that elicit bounce-back responses:

- Tell us about one of your best memories from your days at [Name of Organization].
- The first 50 people to send in correct answers to the following questions will receive a complimentary gift.
- Do you have answers to these trivia questions about [Name of Organization]?
- We're taking a vote. Tell us your stand on the topic of....
- We're looking for examples of.... If you can help, please let us know.
- Do you have news to share for the next issue of our newsletter/magazine? If so, please complete this form.

Boost Your Appeal Response Rate

Standard operating procedure: Send a mass appeal and hope people will give.

Idea to kick up your response rate: Identify persons on your list with the greatest capacity for a generous gift, then follow up on those names with a phone call within a few weeks of mailing the appeal.

The number of recipients to earmark for a phone call depends on the number of people available to make the calls. Count on one person being responsible for 10 to 20 calls and use staff and/or volunteers to figure out a practical number of phone call attempts that can be completed within two weeks of the mailing having been sent.

EXAMPLES FROM WHICH TO LEARN

Being able to see which direct mail tactics have been successful for fellow nonprofits gives your organization the chance to borrow and tweak that idea to a profitable direct mail appeal for your cause. This chapter highlights some unique and successful direct mail appeals used by fellow nonprofits.

Monthly Letter Serves as Relationship-builder, Indirect Solicitation

Officials at Noon Day Ministries (Albuquerque, NM), an organization that serves the homeless, send appeal letters to their mailing list once a month — but these are no ordinary appeal letters. They're much more.

Just as her father did when he began Noon Day Ministries 20 years ago, Ruthie Horn Robbins, board co-chair, sends a one-page letter to the organization's donors and potential donors in which she simply shares her observations on life and the homeless, mixing in Bible verse along the way. Enclosed with the letter is a No. 6-size return envelope.

This simple, no-pressure letter sent to the organization's mailing list of 2,200 brings in about $20,000 each month from an average of 175 donors. Most gifts are under $100. While they occasionally receive larger gifts of about $5,000, and bequests, Robbins says the organization survives on these smaller gifts.

The secret to their success is the relationship-building aspect of the letter. Although it is a mass-produced form letter, it's written in an informal, "friend-to-friend" style that makes readers feel it's written directly to them. "A lot of people write back to me, thanking me for writing about certain things," says Robbins. "One woman I talked to recently said she 'just loved' my last letter."

Susan Walton, development director, Sandia Prep School (Albuquerque, NM), says she likes to receive Noon Day Ministries' monthly letters. "I always read that letter addressed to 'Dear Friend,'" she says. "I contribute once or twice a year. I'm never offended by the letters. Why? It might be a combination of their simplicity, sincerity and lack of mass production feel."

Source: Ruthie Horn Robbins, Board Co-Chair, Noon Day Ministries, Albuquerque, NM. Phone (505) 255- 9265.
E-mail: drmrobb@worldnet.att.net
Susan Walton, Development Director, Sandia Prep School, Albuquerque, NM. Phone (505) 344-1671.
E-mail: swalton@sandiaprep.org

Direct Mail Tip

Recognize that your appeal letter is intended to sell something.

Although direct mail fundraising is different from businesses that are trying to sell products, donors who contribute to a cause through direct mail are also making a purchase — one that is priceless compared to any tangible product. Direct mail donors are purchasing an improved quality of life, a bit of immortality and acts of kindness.

Content not available in this edition

EXAMPLES FROM WHICH TO LEARN

Creative Solicitation Draws Donors

Philabundance, a food rescue organization in Philadelphia, PA, has seen an increase in gifts from renewals and acquisitions by using a brown bag appeal that draws attention to both the mailing and the organization's mission.

The sealed brown paper lunch bag serves as the envelope, not for the appeal letter, but for the reply card and return envelope. The appeal letter is printed right on the back of the bag.

"The appeal not only gets noticed when someone opens their mailbox, it gets across the fact that the organization is trying to feed people," says Eleanor Missimer, director of annual giving.

The organization's brown bag appeal is sent for the fall renewal and acquisition, says Missimer.

"We see an 8 to 10.5 percent return on renewals, and a 1.3 to 1.5 percent return on acquisitions," she says. The average gift for renewals is $45 to $55, while the average gift for acquisitions is $30 to $35.

Source: Eleanor Missimer, Director of Annual Giving, Philabundance, Philadelphia, PA. Phone (215) 339-0900, ext. 269.

Content not available in this edition

Getting Away With Multiple Appeals to the Same Prospects

Would you like to send multiple appeals to the same prospects in the same fiscal year, but worry that doing so might irritate them? Perhaps your concern is unwarranted.

Kelly Brault, assistant director of annual giving, University of Detroit Mercy (Detroit, MI), says she sends multiple appeals until the prospect gives, and doesn't worry too much about irritating prospects. "Your average response rate on a good direct mail is 2 to 5 percent, and contact percentages in telemarketing are so low, sending multiple appeals is just playing the odds and hoping that something will stick," she says. "At the very least, it's reminding alums that you exist."

Brault shares this tip for sending multiple appeals to the same prospects: Mix your soliciting vehicle to get the most out of your participation. She starts with a postcard, then uses a No. 10 envelope, then a phone call and then a self-mailer before going back to prospects with another No. 10.

Gary Brienzo, communications manager, National Arbor Day Foundation (Lincoln, NE), says they contact new prospective members directly up to three times a year, with a policy not to contact anyone in this group more than three times over an 18-month period.

Brienzo shares this tip for sending multiple appeals to the same prospects: Repackage subsequent appeals, referencing past appeals.

Source: Kelly Brault, Assistant Director of Annual Giving, University of Detroit Mercy, Detroit, MI. Phone (313) 578-0326.
E-mail: braultke@udmercy.edu
Gary Brienzo, Communications Manager, National Arbor Day Foundation, Lincoln, NE. Phone (402) 474-5655.
E-mail: gbrienzo@arborday.org

Direct Mail Tips

1. If your goal is to build your donor base, ask for small gifts from new prospects.

2. Use matching challenges to increase your response rate.

3. When seeking a medium-sized gift, say $500 to $2,000, try using a mini-proposal which includes a personalized letter and a one-page project summary.

EXAMPLES FROM WHICH TO LEARN

Personalized Message
Makes for Direct Mail Appeal Success

An appeal with a simple tagline, "Then, Now and Again," has yielded the best results in direct mail campaign history for the Hebrew Academy of Tidewater/Strelitz Early Childhood Center (Virginia Beach, VA).

Eilene Rosenblum, director of development, says each piece of the direct mail appeal is a four-fold, 5 1/2 X 9-inch brochure featuring a school year photo of a donor juxtaposed with a present family photo (where the children are the current students).

"The personalized appeal resonated with recipients not only because they recognized themselves, but because they recognized their contemporaries."

A quote from the donor expressing gratitude for life lessons learned at the academy is featured under the family photo, with information on his/her subsequent education.

The brochure's next two pages feature text on the school's mission and need for financial support, mixed with photos of students who attend the K-6 and preschool division.

Mailed in three parts — August, December and April — the direct mail appeal was sent to 3,000 donors and prospective donors.

Unlike past years when donors who contributed after the first mailing were not sent additional mailings, Rosenblum says all 3,000 persons on the list received all three mailings, plus a thank-you note if they donated, so they could see the complete campaign.

This tactic — along with the use of former students at the center of the appeal's message — proved a winning combination, bringing in 500 gifts totaling more than $350,000. The average gift was $500 and the largest, $2,500.

"This approach yielded the best results for a direct mail appeal we have ever produced," says Rosenblum, pointing to the $50,000 increase in gifts over the prior year's annual campaign. "The personalized appeal resonated with recipients not only because they recognized themselves, but because they recognized their contemporaries. It also resonated with older people who saw their children or their children's children following in their footsteps."

Rosenblum says the mailing was such a success she is using it again for the upcoming year, featuring new participants and their families.

Source: Eilene Rosenblum, Director of Development, Hebrew Academy of Tidewater/Strelitz Early Childhood Center, Virginia Beach, VA.
Phone (757) 424-4327.
E-mail:
Ehrosenblum@hebrewacademy.net

Juxtaposing a past class picture with the student today proved successful for a direct mail appeal for the Hebrew Academy of Tidewater/Strelitz Early Childhood Center (Virginia Beach, VA):

Recognize 'Lifetime Value' in Evaluating Results

It's important to recognize that just because a direct mail nets a less-than-hoped-for amount of gift revenue, that doesn't mean it was a failure. It's important to take the "lifetime value" of donors into account when judging results.

While you may actually lose money in acquiring a new donor, the majority of contributors will probably become repeat givers. That's why it's important to determine the average lifetime value of your donor pool.

Direct Mail Idea

■ To bring in additional revenue, add a checkoff box (similar to the one found on federal tax forms) to all bounce backs. Use it to invite senders to make an additional gift for a specific project.

Content not available in this edition

EXAMPLES FROM WHICH TO LEARN

Gift Asks Combine New Brochures, Personalized Solicitations

To go beyond the traditional gift request letter, staff with the office of development and alumni relations, Sewickley Academy (Sewickley, PA) developed an annual fund series of three brochures — one for each season that falls during the school year.

The tri-fold brochures each fold out to a 20 3/4 X 6-inch, full-color piece that draws prospective donors in with vibrant colors, powerful photographs, personalized solicitations and motivating text.

Paula Dillig, director of development, says they sent 5,500 brochures to alumni, parents, trustees, grandparents and friends of the academy. They personalized each mailing by inserting a 5 X 5-inch card with a message to the constituent receiving it.

The personalized message asked for a donation amount based on information gathered by a database screening of constituents. The message included a postscript reminding the donor that corporate matching gifts were an easy way to double or triple their gift, and how to search the academy website to learn if their company qualified.

Dillig says the annual fund series' goal was threefold: to increase number of donors, increase total given and increase average gift per donor.

In 2006-2007 — the effort's first year — the academy saw individual donors increase by 122 persons over the previous year, Dillig says. "We feel this gives us a great opportunity to build on that and increase the amount of gifts from those individuals."

They plan to build upon those efforts by continuing the annual fund series campaign in the 2007-2008 school year.

Source: Paula Dillig, Director of Development, Sewickley Academy, Sewickley, PA. Phone (412) 741-2230. E-mail: pdillig@swickley.edu

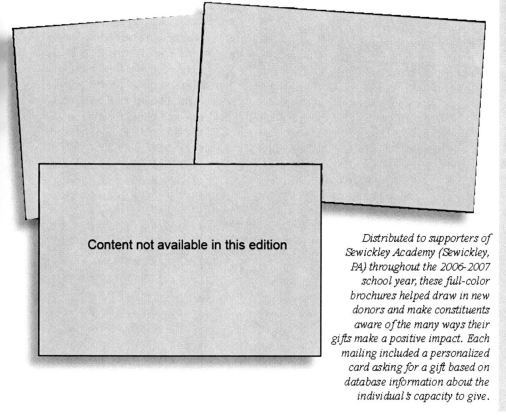

Content not available in this edition

Distributed to supporters of Sewickley Academy (Sewickley, PA) throughout the 2006-2007 school year, these full-color brochures helped draw in new donors and make constituents aware of the many ways their gifts make a positive impact. Each mailing included a personalized card asking for a gift based on database information about the individual's capacity to give.

Holiday Card Serves As Last-minute Appeal

Has your organization considered making a holiday card program a part of your annual fund solicitation efforts?

California Institute of Technology (Caltech) of Pasadena, CA, uses customized holiday cards to symbolize the institution's uniqueness while making a soft gift appeal for the past nine years.

Andy Sudol, director of annual giving programs, says this effort served as a gentle, last-minute reminder to Caltech's main solicitation effort earlier in the year. The program is one of four mailings sent annually.

"At the end of the year, many people are looking at their philanthropic choices and this card serves as another reminder from Caltech that their donation would serve the institution's needs," says Sudol.

The 2006 effort, which distributed 15,000 cards and reply envelopes to Caltech's alumni and parents of current students, generated $15,000. The median gift size received was $100.

The 7 X 5 1/4-inch card featured an image derived from the Palomar-Quest digital sky survey. "Because Caltech is a very internationally diverse community, we wanted to consider the sensitivities of our community and avoid any religious messages. We decided to stick with one of the things Caltech is known for — which was astronomy," says Sudol.

Source: Andy Sudol, Director of Annual Giving Programs, California Institute of Technology, Pasadena, CA. Phone (626) 395-6290. E-mail: asudol@caltech.edu

EXAMPLES FROM WHICH TO LEARN

Long-time Organization's First Appeal a Success

Officials with The Mary Wade Home, a health care facility for the elderly (New Haven, CT), had never had to do formal fundraising until a few years ago when a strategic plan identified several needs that couldn't be met by current funding.

The 136-year-old organization has a healthy endowment and regularly receives unsolicited bequests, says Walter Gaffney, who was hired to head the newly created development office. But, he says, the organization didn't have the funds for specific projects such as holiday gifts for those who are alone, scholarships for staff advancement, furnishings for the residential care wing or weekend transportation.

"The board occasionally sent letters asking for gifts for special projects, but this past year I decided to create a formal direct mail appeal," says Gaffney.

The organization's first annual appeal letter was sent to a mailing list of 830 former donors, patients' family members, vendors and others. Ninety-five people — more than 11 percent — responded with a gift, generating $39,000. The largest gift was $20,000; many others were between $50 and $100. Along with the letter was a gift card that listed several needs and suggested donation amounts for each. Most people chose to designate their gift to those areas, he says.

"We have touched relatives of clients and I think they were happy to give back," says Gaffney.

Source: Walter Gaffney, Advancement Director, The Mary Wade Home, New Haven, CT. Phone (203) 785-8214. E-mail: wgaffney@marywade.org

Content not available in this edition

Content not available in this edition

Content not available in this edition

Content not available in this edition

Postcard Encourages Giving for Honor Roll

What steps do you take to keep supporters informed and enthusiastic about ongoing gift opportunities?

Each spring, alumnae of Simmons College (Boston, MA) receive a 5 X 7-inch postcard that gives them a chance to make a gift and get their name included in their class's Honor Roll of Donors, a class fundraising letter.

The four-color postcard, shown below, features current undergraduate students and a professor with a header that says, "They Are The Simmons Fund." At the bottom, it says, "Won't YOU Be Too? Make your gift by February 15 to be named in your class's Honor Roll of Donors."

Simmons staff sent the postcard to 16,000 undergraduate alumnae who had not yet given in the 2007 fiscal year.

"The design is a continuation of our annual direct mail campaign messaging and brand," says Julianne Silva, associate director, The Simmons Fund.

The campaign began in 2006 and includes photos of students, faculty, staff and alumni and a case for support of The Simmons Fund — the college's annual fund.

The back of the postcard directs alumnae to make their gift online, by phone or by mail. Alums who make gifts by mail are asked to include a specific tracking code on the check's memo line. The appeal code generated $11,383 in its first year.

Source: Julianne Silva, Associate Director, The Simmons Fund, Simmons College, Boston, MA. Phone (617) 521-2342. E-mail: julianne.silva@ simmons.edu

EXAMPLES FROM WHICH TO LEARN

New Direct Mail Package
Helps to Increase Number of Contributors

Mayo Foundation's new donor prospects weren't responding to the conservative message running throughout the Rochester, Minnesota organization's previous direct mail packages, so foundation officials decided to try something new. Recently they revamped their direct mail package to create a more informal look; hired a professional writer to draft a more persuasive, compelling message; and tested the use of personalized address labels.

The approach worked: The new direct mail test package brought in 9,865 new donors, compared to the previous year's 2,494 new donors. Sue Johnson, direct mail manager, says the new direct mail package was designed to be competitive, with a strong message for giving to Mayo. The new package also uses more personalization and is signed by the foundation's medical director of development.

Here's how the foundation's new donor acquisition program (responsible for the acquisition of new donors, renewal of donors and cultivation of donors via direct mail) works, says Bailey:

- Non-donor prospects are solicited four times per year for four years after becoming a patient at Mayo (in accordance with HIPAA regulations, only a patient's name and demographics are shared with the development department).

- If they don't respond, prospects are dropped from the database. Those individuals are then added to the program with a next patient visit.

Source: Sue A. Johnson, Direct Mail Manager, Mayo Foundation, Rochester, MN. Phone (507) 284-5996. E-mail: johnson.sue@mayo.edu

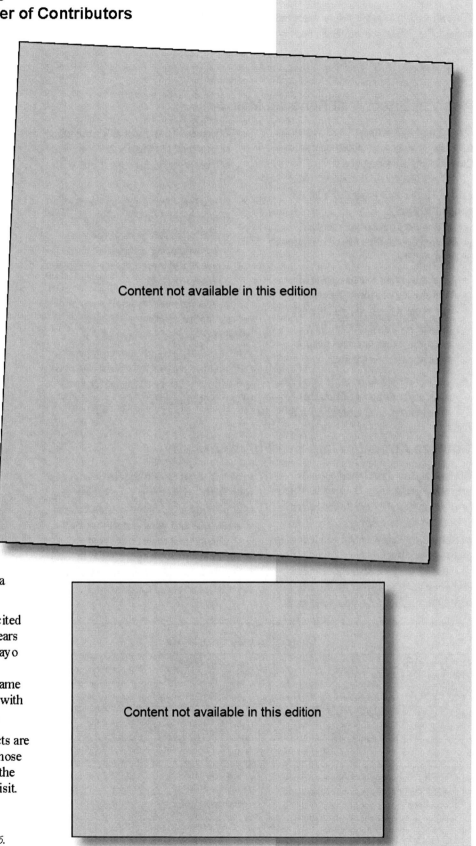

Content not available in this edition

Content not available in this edition

Profitable Direct Mail Appeals: Planning, Implementing and Maximizing Results, Second Edition.
Edited by Scott C. Stevenson.
© 2009 Stevenson, Inc. Published 2009 by Stevenson, Inc.

EVALUATION SHOULD BE ONGOING

The only way to improve future direct mail results is by tracking and evaluating each appeal. The following articles and management tools will help you better measure your results.

Analyze Direct Mail Renewal Methods

Once you have acquired a fit via direct mail, how do you go about renewing the gift the following year?

Does the donor receive a "Dear Friend" letter that is part of a larger general appeal?

Consider these points as you evaluate the best direct mail methods of renewing gifts:

- **Personalized versus general.** Whenever possible, it pays to generate a personalized appeal. Doing so shows donors you recognize they are real people making very real gifts.

- **Anniversary appeal.** If possible, solicit the donor's gift on the anniversary of the previous gift.

If you invite support at a time that works best for the donor, your odds of receiving an increased gift will improve.

- **State last year's gift amount.** Remind the donor of what was contributed last year. It conveys your awareness of their level of support and encourages a similar or increased gift.

If you represent a small shop and cannot justify sending personalized appeals on the anniversary of the previous gift, send groups of appeals out monthly or quarterly. That way you are still responding to the anniversary of the previous gift.

Analyze Appeal to Improve Future Results

Which of your direct mail appeals was most productive last year? Which resulted in the greatest dollar return? What was the average gift size from each mailing? How much did it cost to raise each dollar?

It makes good sense to monitor and analyze your direct mail costs and results throughout the course of each

year and prior to drafting an operational plan for the upcoming year. Doing so will provide a quantitative measure of what works and what doesn't work.

Complete a direct mail cost analysis report (example shown below) to track costs and results of solicitation appeals throughout the year.

Measure Your Direct Mail ROI

How do you calculate the ROI (return on investment) each time you send an appeal letter to a group of would-be contributors?

While there may be a number of factors you could consider (e.g., average size gift, total gifts raised, number of first-time gifts), the ROI is generally the number generated by dividing total profit of the mailing by the mailing's total cost.

Here are a few ways of calculating ROI:

- A. Number of pieces mailed multiplied by:
- B. Percent response rate multiplied by:
- C. Average gift amount multiplied by:
- D. Percentage of profit per gift.
- E. Subtract this amount from total cost of the mailing for your ROI.

Know Your Cost Per Response

There are various ways of measuring a mailing's success.

For instance, after completing a direct mail appeal, you can use cost per response (CPR) as one way to measure its success against other mailings.

The CPR is determined by simply adding all promotion costs and dividing it by the number of gifts received. Some organizations include up-front costs only (printing, postage, list rental, etc.) while others include subsequent costs (thank-you letters, receipts, etc.) in determining the overall CPR.

Direct Mail Cost Analysis

Appeal No.: _____ Average Gift: _____
Target Audience: _____ Largest Gift: _____
Drop Date: _____ First-time Gifts: _____

Total Quantity	Total Cost	Unit Cost	Total Responses	Response Rate	Total Gifts	Net	Cost to Raise $1

Appeal No.: _____ Average Gift: _____
Target Audience: _____ Largest Gift: _____
Drop Date: _____ First-time Gifts: _____

Total Quantity	Total Cost	Unit Cost	Total Responses	Response Rate	Total Gifts	Net	Cost to Raise $1

EVALUATION SHOULD BE ONGOING

RFM Formula Measures Direct Mail Success

Many nonprofits use the RFM (recency, frequency and monetary) formula to target their direct mailings to donors most likely to give. No special, expensive software is needed. It's simple, saves mailing costs and increases response rates.

RFM allows you to determine which donors are interested and target them by examining how recently they gave (recency), how often they give (frequency) and how much they give (monetary). If your organization has donors' giving histories on file, you can do an RFM analysis.

How it works:

Step 1: For each of the three categories, rank donors in descending order (e.g., one through five). For recency, rank donors in order by the date of their most recent gift; donors who gave recently get higher recency scores (e.g., the top 20 percent get fives, next 20 percent get fours, etc.). For frequency, determine the number

of gifts each donor has given during a certain time frame; donors who gave more often receive higher frequency scores. For monetary, determine each donor's average gift size; the bigger the amount, the higher the score.

Step 2: Donors now have a RFM score (e.g., a donor with a 3-5-1 score gives frequent small gifts). These RFM scores allow you to target mailings to donors more effectively and strategically, instead of just to your entire list.

Cautions:

- Do not over-solicit donors with the highest RFM scores.
- Donors with low scores should not be neglected, but cultivated.
- Make sure to monitor periodically and recalculate RFM scores after mailings.

Direct Mail Tip

- Appeals should be tailored for each of the following groups: donors, lapsed donors and nondonors. You may choose to further segment each of those groups and develop an even more targeted message.

Assess Direct Mail Contact Frequency

If your organization recently concluded its fiscal year, take time to analyze the various direct mail contacts you plan to have with your constituency throughout the upcoming year.

Do various mailings complement one another? Are they spaced evenly? Are they conveying intended messages at appropriate times?

Now is the time to coordinate these key communications pieces.

Track Each Direct Mail Appeal's Success

Before you send out that direct mail package, be sure to develop a method to track its success, says Sarah Clifton, development coordinator, The Fund for Animals (Silver Spring, MD). For smaller organizations just starting out in direct mail, a simple chart can help track a direct mail solicitation's success, she says. Here's what data to collect:

- What percentage of individuals

solicited responded with a gift?
- What was the average dollar amount given?
- What was the total cost of the package per dollar raised?
- What was the total cost spent per new donor acquired through the mailing?
- What was the total financial gain or loss of the mailing?

By collecting this information, says Clifton, you can create a chart that helps you see how much money you spent, how each list performed comparatively, and how much it cost to acquire each donor.

Source: Sarah Clifton, Development Coordinator, The Fund for Animals, Silver Spring, MD. E-mail: sclifton@fund.org

Package Code	# Solicited	# Responses	% Responses	Total Raised	Average Gift	Total Cost	Cost/package	Income/ package	Cost/dollar raised	Net Income
SampleA-02	500	6	1.2	$108.00	$18.00	$250	$.50	$0.22	$2.31	($142.00)
SampleB-02	500	15	3	$120.00	$8.00	$320.00	$0.64	$0.24	$2.67	($200.00)
SampleC-02	500	8	1.6	$215.00	$26.88	$225.00	$0.45	$0.43	$1.05	($10.00)
SampleD-02	500	1	0.2	$15.00	$15.00	$200.00	$0.40	$0.03	$13.33	($185.00)

EVALUATION SHOULD BE ONGOING

It Pays to Conduct Direct Mail Cost Analysis

Which of your direct mail appeals was most productive last year? Which resulted in the greatest dollar return? What was the average gift size from each mailing? How much did it cost to raise each dollar?

It's wise to analyze your direct mail costs and results throughout the course of each year. Doing so will provide a quantitative measure of what works and what doesn't work. It will also help shape plans for future mailings.

Using a direct mail cost analysis form such as the one at right can help track costs and results of solicitation appeals throughout the year. The results from this simple tool should be included in your annual operational plan.

2008 Direct Mail Cost Analysis

Appeal No.: _____

Audience: _____

Mailing Date: _____   Average Gift: _____

Total Quantity	Total Cost	Unit Cost	Total Responses	Response Rate	Total Gifts	Cost to Net Raise $1

Appeal No.: _____

Audience: _____

Mailing Date: _____   Average Gift: _____

Total Quantity	Total Cost	Unit Cost	Total Responses	Response Rate	Total Gifts	Cost to Net Raise $1

Appeal No.: _____

Audience: _____

Mailing Date: _____   Average Gift: _____

Total Quantity	Total Cost	Unit Cost	Total Responses	Response Rate	Total Gifts	Cost to Net Raise $1

Appeal No.: _____

Audience: _____

Mailing Date: _____   Average Gift: _____

Total Quantity	Total Cost	Unit Cost	Total Responses	Response Rate	Total Gifts	Cost to Net Raise $1

Definitions

Total Quantity: Total number of pieces mailed.

Total Cost: Entire cost of direct mail appeal (i.e., list acquisition, printing, postage, etc.)

Unit Cost: Total cost to execute effort (including postage), divided by total quantity.

Total Responses: Cumulative number of gifts received.

Response Rate: Total responses divided by total quantity.

Total Gifts: Total dollar amount generated by the appeal.

Net: Total cost divided by the total gifts.

Cost to Raise a Dollar: Total cost divided by total gifts.

Average Gift: Total gift amount generated divided by total responses.

Profitable Direct Mail Appeals: Planning, Implementing and Maximizing Results, Second Edition.
Edited by Scott C. Stevenson.
© 2009 Stevenson, Inc. Published 2009 by Stevenson, Inc.

PLANNING WORKSHEET

Organization _____

Fiscal Year Begins _____ Ends _____

Historical Data From Most Recent Fiscal Year

Total gross direct mail revenue $ _____

Total net direct mail gift revenue $ _____

Cost to revenue ratio _____

Total number of appeals for past year _____

Dates	Audience	Quantity	Response

Upcoming Year's Goals

Projected total direct mail revenue $ _____

Dates	Audience	Quantity	Response

PLANNING WORKSHEET

Additional Goals/Considerations for Current Year Appeals

Annual Fund Theme _____

Primary Appeal Message _____

_____

Secondary Messages   1. _____

                                         2. _____

                                         3. _____

Printed Materials to Be Developed for Each Appeal

Package Components

Mailing No. 1   _____   _____

                             _____   _____

Mailing No. 2   _____   _____

                             _____   _____

Mailing No. 3   _____   _____

                             _____   _____

Mailing No. 4   _____   _____

                             _____   _____

Mailing No. 5   _____   _____

                             _____   _____

Mailing No. 6   _____   _____

                             _____   _____

Mailing No. 7   _____   _____

                             _____   _____